IF GOD HAD A FRIDGE,

YOUR PICTURE WOULD BE ON IT!

Self-Image:
How seeing yourself as God sees you
changes everything

D1409115

GLYN NORMAN

CONTENTS

GLYN NORMAN

DEDICATION

To my mother Veronica, who taught me to believe that I could accomplish anything I set my mind to.

To my wife Cathleen, and my children, Landon and Cicely – I love you with all my heart

GLYN NORMAN

ACKNOWLEDGMENTS

Thanks to Karen L., Ann M., and particularly, Christina N. who read early versions of this manuscript and made numerous helpful suggestions

Thanks to Steve Hill, for his proofreading prowess – any errors that remain are mine

Thanks to Kelly Nielsen for his superb cover design and interior formatting.

And finally, my thanks to my Lord and Savior Jesus Christ, who presents me "without fault, and with great joy." (Jude v24)

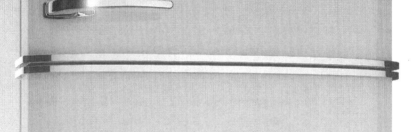

CHAPTER

1

DOES ANYBODY EVEN WANT ME HERE?

Setting the Scene

I was 14 years old, sitting in the classroom waiting for class to start. One of the popular boys in class, Philip, was due to leave town the next week, moving with his parents to a far-off city in the north of England. The others in the "cool" group were gathered around him, because he was sharing his new address with those who wanted to write to him. I sat a few rows away, and also wrote down the address. We hadn't been the closest of friends, but I thought I might want to write.

Suddenly, one of the cool kids turned around, pointed at me and said, "Look, Half-Pint is writing it down." How they laughed. How they laughed at the very idea that their cool friend might want to get a letter from me, or even more hilarious, that he might want to write back. My face suffused with red shame, and I quietly put my pen and paper away. How foolish of me. How awkward and silly and embarrassing for me to dare count myself among his friends. I didn't show much expression, but inside I was crushed.

I realized that "Half-Pint" did not belong in this circle. That nickname was given to me because of my diminutive size (my body took a time out from growing at age 10 and didn't start up again until I was 13), and was just one of many that they used. Suffice it to say, I got the message. What was clearly reflected back to me was that I didn't belong. I had a social status, but it was far below that of these cool ones.

———

I don't make it a habit to watch scary films, but from my childhood, I think I remember more than one with a plot along these lines ...

A couple become stranded as their car runs out of fuel on a lonely forest road. They seek shelter at a Gothic mansion, where the door is opened by an old, old man who is willing to let them stay there for the night. As they make their way up the stairs to their room, the man issues a dire warning:

"Just one thing I ask ... whatever you do, do not go into the West Wing. There are things there ..." he never completes his sentence, his utterance seeming to have tired him. He waves his arm twice toward the stairway in dismissal and wanders down a dark corridor to his own room.

With trepidation, the couple ascends the stairs, finds their rooms and prepare for bed, though neither feels particularly sleepy after the dire warning.

———

And you, dear reader, know how the story continues. Foolishly, they do not heed the old man's advice. They hear noises and wander off to investigate the source, ending up in the West Wing, where they discover the old man's hideously deformed relative, whom he keeps hidden from the world. They run and trip as the drooling maniac stumbles toward them, his zombie-like gait never slowing ... you get the picture.

The message of this book is simply this: you are not the hideously deformed relative in the house that needs to be hidden away. You are not the one who slipped in, hoping your entrance wouldn't get noticed, while all the good people were being admitted. You are not the sum of the opinions, judgments, criticisms, sarcasm, looks and comments of others. You are not the sum of your parents, your education, your job, society or any other source.

For most of us, our self-image is like what we see when we walk through a hall of mirrors. At every turn, a different version of ourselves is reflected back to us: thinner, fatter, distorted. In a carnival, it is funny - in life, it is tragic. We find ourselves compromised in our ability to love ourselves and to love others.

How many of us suffer in our relationships, in our view of ourselves and our potential, because we have been presented with a distorted image?

- Maybe a parent made you feel unloved and unwanted.
- Maybe a teacher convinced you that you would never amount to anything.
- Perhaps a boss let you know how little he thought of you.
- Maybe you have been abused and sinned against, and you feel dirty and ashamed.
- Perhaps a spouse has chipped away at your self-belief, and you feel like a failure.
- Perhaps the weight of your own mistakes and poor choices weighs on you daily.
- Maybe you became persuaded that if you were just a little prettier, a little smarter, a little less socially awkward, then you would be acceptable.

Over the years I have been a pastor, through hundreds of counseling appointments and pastoral conversations, I have seen the same issues surface again and again, with a common root cause: We look to the wrong places for our self-image.

Only when we understand how God sees us will we experience freedom. Understanding how we appear to God changes everything. Only when we appreciate to the depths of our being how precious and loved we are by our Creator and Savior can we truly move into the abundant life that he promised us.

In this book, I will examine different sources of our self-image and show you that you have a unique value to God, a special place in his plan. As the title says, "If God had a fridge, your picture would be on it!"

Don't leave yourself crippled emotionally, spiritually and psychologically. You deserve better and those who live and work with you certainly deserve better. Understand who you really are, shatter the shackles of toxic self-image and replace them with a view of yourself that will truly set you free to be all God intended you to be.

Don't wait any longer. Turn the page now, and start your discovery to a whole, new you.

GLYN NORMAN

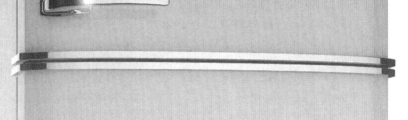

CHAPTER
2

WHAT DOES JESUS TEACH US ABOUT SELF-IMAGE?

What was Jesus' emotional and psychological state of health, and why?

You would think that Jesus escapes the normal demands of psychological and emotional health. After all, he is the Son of God and the most perfect human being ever to walk the earth. But remember that as much as he is God, he is also fully human, and as such, has the same emotional and psychological wiring as you and I. That means he actually has the same needs we do, and if they were not met, he would suffer just the same. As we look at Jesus, we will see that he is healthy in all regards: he knew where he came from, he felt secure in himself, and he knew what his purpose was.

In this chapter we are going to explore the three key components of Jesus' healthy self-image, see how they were built, and understand why we have a desperate need for those same components in our life.

To demonstrate the depths of Jesus' psychological and emotional health, we are going to examine a scene, recorded in the Gospel of John, chapter 13, from near the end of his earthly life.

Jesus Washes the Disciples' Feet

1 It was just before the Passover Feast. Jesus knew that the time had come for him to leave this world and go to the Father. Having loved his own who were in the world, he now showed them the full extent of his love.

2 The evening meal was being served, and the devil had already prompted Judas Iscariot, son of Simon, to betray Jesus. 3 Jesus knew that the Father had put all things under his power, and that he had come from God and was returning to God; 4 so he got up from the meal, took off his outer clothing, and wrapped a towel around his waist.

5 After that, he poured water into a basin and began to wash his disciples' feet, drying them with the towel that was wrapped around him.

6 he came to Simon Peter, who said to him, "Lord, are you going to wash my feet?"

7 Jesus replied, "You do not realize now what I am doing, but later you will understand."

8 "No," said Peter, "you shall never wash my feet." Jesus answered, "Unless I wash you, you have no part with me."

9 "Then, Lord," Simon Peter replied, "not just my feet but my hands and my head as well!"

10 Jesus answered, "A person who has had a bath needs only to wash his feet; his whole body is clean. And you are clean, though not every one of you." 11 For he knew who was going to betray him, and that was why he said not every one was clean.

12 When he had finished washing their feet, he put on his clothes and returned to his place. "Do you understand what I have done for you?" he asked them. 13 "You call me 'Teacher' and 'Lord,' and rightly so, for that is what I am. 14 Now that I, your Lord and Teacher, have washed your feet, you also should wash one another's feet. 15 I have set you an example that you should do as I have done for you. 16 I tell you the truth, no servant is greater than his master, nor is a messenger greater than the one who sent him. 17 Now that you know these things, you will be blessed if you do them.

Cast your eyes back for a moment to verses 3-5 and note these key phrases:

* Jesus knew that the Father had put all things under his power

Jesus is fully aware and comfortable with his

place in the world, knowing what he can and cannot do.

italic * and that he had come from God
Jesus knows his origin, that he comes from God the Father.

* and was returning to God
Jesus knows his destiny and his destination.

* so ... He wrapped a towel around his waist
Jesus is entirely comfortable serving others, not worried about the low social status that this task implied, since it was usually done by a household servant. He is able to take on a position of humility with no loss of his own self-worth. This is so shocking that Peter, ever the quick-to-speak disciple, objects.

In summary, what we encounter here is a Jesus who is very conscious of his origins, aware and comfortable with his place and role in the world, confident in his final destination, and so secure in his own worth that he does not feel that serving others diminishes him in any way. That is a healthy self-image.

How was Jesus' self-image shaped?

Next, let's look at the ways in which Jesus self-image was shaped.

To start our investigation, we will jump to the scene where Jesus is baptized by John the Baptist.

13 Then Jesus came from Galilee to the Jordan to be baptized by John. 14 But John tried to deter him, saying, "I need to be baptized by you, and do you come to me?"

15 Jesus replied, "Let it be so now; it is proper for us to do this to fulfill all righteousness." Then John consented.

16 As soon as Jesus was baptized, he went up out of the water. At that moment heaven was opened, and he saw the Spirit of God descending like a dove and lighting on him. 17 And a voice from heaven said, "This is my Son, whom I love; with him I am well pleased." (Matthew 3:13-17)

Although this is just a small extract from Scripture, it contains a treasure trove of guidance on the question of self-esteem. Let's break it down:

John tries to deter Jesus, but Jesus insists, and then John complies. John the Baptist was a pretty intimidating character. Clothed in camel hair, with a diet of locusts and honey, John had a reputation as a straight-speaking prophet who would not be trifled with; yet Jesus has no hesitation in directing John to do what he asked. I think this reveals a pretty strong sense of self, and perhaps an even stronger sense of destiny. Jesus knows that he needs to be baptized "in order to fulfill all righteousness," i.e., to keep in line with what God wants from his life. He seems secure in his identity and purpose.

Then comes the voice from heaven, the voice of the Father: "This is my Son, whom I love; with him I am well pleased." Contained within those 13 words are the basic building blocks of healthy self-esteem:

Identity: *This is my Son* – The Father acknowledges and is publicly proud of his parental connection with Jesus. For Jesus, he hears his Father "own" him with pride. He hears his Father unashamed to declare their relationship. There is no embarrassment or hesitation.

Love: *Whom I love* – The Father is not distant or removed, or emotionally unengaged. He loves his son, and he wants the world to hear it. There's no confusion of emotion here. It is simply pure, divine love that is being expressed.

Affirmation: *With him I am well-pleased* - The verdict of the God of the universe on what his Son just did is that he is "well-pleased." What Jesus just did was not merely adequate, just making the passing grade; it caused the Father to be well-pleased. Jesus receives the fatherly affirmation that he needs, given without measure.

The next evidence of the building blocks of Jesus' self-image is found in the event commonly known as the Transfiguration, recorded in all three of the synoptic Gospels. For our purposes, we'll use the version in Matthew 17:

———

1 After six days Jesus took with him Peter, James and John the brother of James, and led them up a high mountain by themselves. 2 There he was transfigured before them. His face shone like the sun, and his clothes became as white as the light. 3 Just then there appeared before them Moses and Elijah, talking with Jesus.

4 Peter said to Jesus, "Lord, it is good for us to be here. If you wish, I will put up three shelters - one for you, one for Moses and one for Elijah."

5 While he was still speaking, a bright cloud enveloped them, and a voice from the cloud said, "This is my Son, whom I love; with him I am well pleased. Listen to him!"

6 When the disciples heard this, they fell facedown to the ground, terrified. 7 But Jesus came and touched them. "Get up," he said. "Don't be afraid." 8 When they looked up, they saw no one except Jesus. (Matthew 17:1-8)

In a speech similar to the one given at Jesus' baptism, the Father again takes the opportunity to affirm the Son:

This is my Son, whom I love; with him I am well pleased. Listen to him!

Identity: *This is my Son* – Again, there is ownership, connection, and an acknowledgment of the special bond between them.

Love: *Whom I love* – Again, we see an outright admission of God's fatherly affection for his Son.

Affirmation: *With him I am well-pleased* – This is another affirmation that Jesus' obedience pleases his Father.

Affirmation: *Listen to him:* – There is a new component here, different from the baptism speech. The command for those present to listen to Jesus also is very affirmative, since it is God's confirmation that Jesus has something important to say, something that should be followed. It is not a stretch to see this as God's statement of belief in Jesus - that he will continue to speak God's way, and that they can do no better than to listen to him. It is as if God is saying, "He's getting it right. Pay close attention! Listen!" If the God of the universe gives you the thumbs up on your communication, that is a powerful affirmation.

Our last stop on this lightning tour will be a very brief excursion to an incident that happened when

Jesus was only 12 years old. This story does not so much show the *shaping* of Jesus' self-image as much as *evidence* of what was already there, even at this tender age, because of his sense of being important to God:

> *41 Every year his parents went to Jerusalem for the Feast of the Passover. 42 When he was twelve years old, they went up to the Feast, according to the custom. 43 After the Feast was over, while his parents were returning home, the boy Jesus stayed behind in Jerusalem, but they were unaware of it. 44 Thinking he was in their company, they traveled on for a day. Then they began looking for him among their relatives and friends. 45 When they did not find him, they went back to Jerusalem to look for him. 46 After three days they found him in the temple courts, sitting among the teachers, listening to them and asking them questions. 47 Everyone who heard him was amazed at his understanding and his answers. 48 When his parents saw him, they were astonished. His mother said to him, "Son, why have you treated us like this? your father and I have been anxiously searching for you."*

> *49 "Why were you searching for me?" he asked. "Didn't you know I had to be in my Father's house?" 50 But they did not understand what he was saying to them.*

> *51 Then he went down to Nazareth with them and was obedient to them. But his mother treasured all these things in her heart. 52 And Jesus grew in wisdom and stature, and in favor with God and men. (Luke 2:41-52)*

There are a couple of things to notice here. Being lost would be an alarming situation for most children, but that seems not to be the case with Jesus. He is happily debating and chatting with the teachers in the Temple courts. His answer to his parents' query is telling:

Didn't you know I had to be in my Father's house?

First-century Jews were not in the habit of calling God "my Father," and the fact that Jesus uses that phrase suggests that he senses a close intimacy and bond with God, beyond that normally experienced by others. We could conclude that Jesus isn't alarmed about being lost because he is, in a sense, not lost at all; he is in his "Father's house." The bond and connection that he feels with his heavenly Father is sufficient to overcome the loss or absence of his earthly parents, Mary his mother and Joseph, his adoptive father. He has an awareness of his relationship with the heavenly Father that others simply do not comprehend fully at this point - thus, the statement in verse 5 that "they did not understand."

Another indicator of Jesus' overall health comes in verse 52, which states that "Jesus grew in wisdom and stature, and in favor with God and men." Jesus' development as a child encompassed the mental ("wisdom"), physical ("stature"), spiritual ("favor with God") and relational/social ("favor with ... men").

Perhaps the last clue to the significance of a proper sense of our identity is found in the temptation narrative from the book of Matthew:

1 Then Jesus was led by the Spirit into the desert to be tempted by the devil. 2 After fasting forty days and forty nights, he was hungry. 3 The tempter came to him and said, "If you are the Son of God, tell these stones to become bread."

4 Jesus answered, "It is written: 'Man does not live on bread alone, but on every word that comes from the mouth of God.'"

5 Then the devil took him to the holy city and had him stand on the highest point of the temple. 6 "If you are the Son of God," he said, "throw yourself down. For it is written:

"'He will command his angels concerning you,
*   and they will lift you up in their hands,*
so that you will not strike your foot against a stone.'"
7 Jesus answered him, "It is also written: 'Do not put the Lord your God to the test.'"

8 Again, the devil took him to a very high mountain and showed him all the kingdoms of the world and their splendor. 9 "All this I will give you," he said, "if you will bow down and worship me."

10 Jesus said to him, "Away from me, Satan! For it is written: 'Worship the Lord your God, and serve him only.'"

11 Then the devil left him, and angels came and attended him.

Did you see it? In both verse 3 and verse 6, Satan starts his challenge with "If you are the Son of God …" It is a direct attack on Jesus' identity. The enemy seeks to make Jesus question his identity and then prove it in an illegitimate manner. He does that because he knows that this is the core of our being, and more than anything else, influences how we think and act.

If the enemy successfully assails us in the area of

our identity, he can neutralize us, and make it ever more likely that we will fail to understand our value, significance, and usefulness to God. For Jesus, just as for us, a right perspective on identity is key.

What does this reveal about our needs, and what happens if those needs aren't met?

The logical conclusion to all this is that just like Jesus, we have certain elements that are supposed to make up the building blocks of our self-image. Knowing that we were wanted before we ever entered this world, knowing that we are loved by our parents, knowing that we have value and a purpose, being affirmed for what we contribute – those are all essential to a healthy view of self.

If we don't get those needs met, then a gaping hole exists in our psyche, and we will try to fill that hole with all manner of things, ranging from the moderately healthy to the extremely damaging. It has become almost a cliché in business, that the most successful individuals are those who are over-achieving in order to try and impress a parent that they failed to impress as a child. In many sad cases, the parent whose affection and affirmation they seek may not even be alive, but there is something within us that longs for the parental "Well done," and a significant deficit is created in us if we don't receive that as children.

When those basic needs are not met, we are forever adrift, trying to establish who we are, in ways that are tenuous and unstable. We might try to fit into the in-crowd, and pay a high price for such acceptance – engaging in behaviors and adhering to value systems that may be very different from who we really are, or want to be. Perhaps we try to impress at school, and being strong academically becomes our defining factor. Perhaps bad behavior gets the attention of our parents more than good behavior ever did, and we are so hungry for attention that even negative attention is better than being ignored.

I wonder if the almost-rabid devotion some sports fans have for their team reveals at its heart a search for identity, a group to be a part of, the opportunity to associate with (hopefully) an entity that wins. Even the language choice, "*We* lost to Notre Dame last night," when the person is no longer at college shows either a legitimate sense of *alma mater* pride or a yearning to hark back to that sense of belonging.

When our need for love is not met, anything that feels like love will do as a substitute until real love comes along. How many young girls give up their virginity to young men who claim they love them, but who then soon move on to the next conquest?

How many men marry the first girl who will sleep with them, because in their limited experience, that is the closest to love they've ever been?

In the absence of genuine love, both men and women will accept sexual intimacy as a substitute. We are hard-wired to desire intimacy, and if we can't get it in legitimate ways, then illegitimate will do.

Teen pregnancy and promiscuous behavior are not caused by illegitimate desires. They are caused by legitimate needs being met in illegitimate ways. In fact, that could be said of almost all sin: it is not that the desires themselves are wrong. It's a question of context.

For many individuals who do not get those needs

met, the pain is immense. Depression, isolation and loneliness can result. Since we naturally seek to avoid pain, we will try to numb it any way we can.

The bottom line is that just like Jesus, we need to have a healthy sense of identity, to know that we are loved, and to be affirmed for who we are.

In this chapter we have seen that Jesus' healthy self-image is made up of the same building blocks that can create a healthy self-image in us. Just as a solid sense of identity, love and affirmation permeated his life, so they need to sink deep into our heart and soul, too.

CHAPTER
3
AM I A COSMIC ACCIDENT?

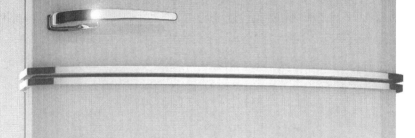

If you have Internet access, click the following link as an introduction to this chapter:

VIDEO LINK: Nick Vujicic
http://www.youtube.com/watch?v=r0daM97RT0k

Since the age of Darwin, it has become very easy to reach the conclusion that we are random products of a chance universe; that we are nothing more than a coincidental collision of atoms that just happened to produce a human being. Although Darwin never foresaw that that conclusion would be reached through his theory, the 20th century inevitably directed people to the conclusion that life can be explained purely through science and that humans hold no particularly special place in the evolutionary system, except that they happen to be more highly evolved than all other species.

There are a number of problems with that view, not least of which is that the major planks of the Darwinian and evolutionary theory are now viewed with skepticism by many respectable scientists. Unfortunately, that has led to a perspective that has diminished the perceived value of human life. That is in stark contrast to the high view of humanity given in the first chapters of the Bible:

> *26 Then God said, "Let us make man in our image, in our likeness, and let them rule over the fish of the sea and the birds of the air, over the livestock, over all the earth, and over all the creatures that move along the ground."*
>
> *27 So God created man in his own image,*

in the image of God he created him;
male and female he created them.
28 God blessed them and said to them, "Be fruitful and
increase in number; fill the earth and subdue it. Rule over
the fish of the sea and the birds of the air and over every
living creature that moves on the ground.
29 Then God said, "I give you every seed-bearing plant on
the face of the whole earth and every tree that has fruit with
seed in it. They will be yours for food. 30 And to all the
beasts of the earth and all the birds of the air and all the
creatures that move on the ground-everything that has the
breath of life in it-I give every green plant for food." And it
was so.

31 God saw all that he had made, and it was very good.
(Genesis 1:26-31)

A parallel account, with a slightly different telling of
the story, is found in Genesis 2:

4 This is the account of the heavens and the earth when they
were created.

When the Lord God made the earth and the heavens - 5
and no shrub of the field had yet appeared on the earth and
no plant of the field had yet sprung up, for the Lord God
had not sent rain on the earth and there was no man to
work the ground, 6 but streams came up from the earth and
watered the whole surface of the ground - 7 the Lord God
formed the man from the dust of the ground and breathed
into his nostrils the breath of life, and the man became a
living being. (Genesis 2:4-7)

Let's look at the significance of this account.
First, verse 26 of Genesis 1 makes it clear that we

are made in the image of God. What does that mean? Well, since God is spirit, and has no physical form (at least not until the Incarnation), it cannot mean physical image. What it can mean is that somehow the image of God is represented in us in some spiritual form, and perhaps emotionally and mentally, too. The ability to connect with the divine, the ability to love and to reason – those are attributes of God that are reflected in us. We are wired to connect with our Creator, and we are made in his image.

Second, humankind is given responsibility over the animal kingdom: We are to "rule." Now, of course, that does not excuse the excesses that the human race has engaged in, such as diminishing some animal populations through hunting or overfishing, but it does show that rather than simply being a more advanced version of the same category (as the evolutionists would have us believe), we belong to a different category. We are more than hairless apes who have become proficient with tools. We are entrusted with the stewardship of the animal kingdom and the planet itself. The inference is that we are something more than random; we are people made in the image of God and entrusted with a task.

Third, notice God's verdict on what he has created. Up to this point, with every element of God's creation prior to humanity, God's assessment is "… it was good." Then suddenly, after humans are created, the assessment jumps to "very good." The addition of human beings to the created order elevated the assessment to "very good." The One who flung stars into space and spun the planets into their orbits, the One who placed galaxies in motion, casts his eyes to these fragile humans and declares them "very good."

Fourth, although God created everything else by a simple spoken command – Let there be light, and there was light, for example – when it comes to the creation of the man, God "formed [him] from the dust of the ground." The word used in the hebrew text implies "by design, with intention." The very word choice militates against the idea that there is anything random or accidental about our creation. God planned it and carried it out – he was "hands on" with the creation of the man – and breathed his life into the man's nostrils. The very breath of God was our first intake, giving us life and filling our lungs.

Let's look at another passage of Scripture, this time from the Psalms:

For you created my inmost being;
you knit me together in my mother's womb.
14 I praise you because I am fearfully and wonderfully made;
your works are wonderful,
I know that full well.
15 My frame was not hidden from you
when I was made in the secret place.
When I was woven together in the depths of the earth,
16 your eyes saw my unformed body.
All the days ordained for me
were written in your book
before one of them came to be. (Psalm 139:13-16)

This psalm, although using language that is primarily poetic rather than biological, makes clear the creative, intentional involvement of God in our creation, even at the embryonic stage. I was "knit together" by God, the sinews, nerves, bones, flesh and even fingerprints arranged in a unique fashion to make me uniquely me. Even identical twins have non-identical DNA. We are, each of us in our own way, unique. We are "fearfully and wonderfully made." I can imagine almost a hush of awe as the psalmist put those words together and considered their implications.

You may not think much of yourself, or view yourself as anything special, but in God's eyes you are "fearfully and wonderfully made" and "very good." There is nothing accidental about you. You are on this earth because God designed you and has a place and a plan for you.

Does my life have meaning?

Since you are here, do you have a purpose? Is there a reason for your life beyond mere existence? Is there more to your being that simply existing because your parents responded to the biological imperative to re-create?

Some modern philosophies would suggest that there is not.

The philosophy of existentialism states basically that there is no inherent meaning to life. Since that realization is almost intolerable, existentialists seek to create meaning – to create a loving family, to protect the planet, or perhaps to engage in some worthy cause. Nihilism takes the idea further, stating that not only is there no inherent meaning, there can not be any meaning, and that any attempt to imbue life on earth with meaning is doomed to failure.

The Bible, on the other hand, declares that we have meaning and purpose:

For we are God's workmanship, created in Christ Jesus to do good works, which God prepared in advance for us to do. (Ephesians 2:10)

What a wonderful verse! It builds upon the idea that we are handcrafted by God. The Amplified Bible makes the affirmation of Ephesians 2:10 even clearer:

10 For we are God's [own] handiwork (His workmanship), recreated in Christ Jesus, [born anew] that we may do those good works which God predestined (planned beforehand) for us [taking paths which he prepared ahead of time], that we should walk in them [living the good life which he prearranged and made ready for us to live].

So, we are God's workmanship, and we are created in Christ Jesus to do good works. The whole idea of being "in Christ Jesus" has deep theological significance, and we'll explore that more later, but for now, notice that there are "good works" for us to do. That means God has things that he has designed for us to do. If we were useless, unwanted or unnecessary, it would not make sense for God to do that. Obviously, he feels that we have a role to play that is significant, and that if we do not play our part, the world will be less because of it. There will be things God wants done that will not get done unless we play our part.

I think that speaks to the deep part of us that longs for significance. We want to know that who we are, and what we do, counts for something. This verse answers that in the absolute affirmative. We are part of God's plan for changing this world, from the state it is currently in to something better.

Even in the dark times of our life when we are feeling down and oppressed, God offers a future of hope. In the Book of Jeremiah, the prophet brings a promise to the people of God, who at that time are exiled and held captive in an enemy nation. God tells them through the prophet that this is not the end of the story, that something good lies ahead:

> *11 For I know the plans I have for you," declares the Lord, "plans to prosper you and not to harm you, plans to give you hope and a future. 12 Then you will call upon me and come and pray to me, and I will listen to you.*
> *(Jeremiah 29:11-12)*

Although this was a promise to a nation, at a particular time of their existence, I don't think it is illegitimate to extrapolate that what God wanted for his people then is what he still wants for people, individuals (including you!) and nations: to experience the hope and future that he has for them.

God wants so much more for us than mere existence. Jesus states in the Gospel of John:

> *I have come that they may have life, and have it to the full.*
> *(John 10:10b)*

That is so encouraging. Jesus does not want us to just putter along, day after day, like mindless drones. He wants us to experience life to the full, in abundance, embracing each day with zeal and enthusiasm as the gift that it is. For many of us, that requires a change of mindset.

I'm reminded of the movie *Groundhog Day*, in which the protagonist wakes up to experience the same day again and again. At first, realizing that his actions have no long-lasting consequences, he becomes recklessly self-indulgent, eating bad food and taking risks with his life. He reaches a point when the emptiness of that approach brings him to despair, and he attempts to commit suicide. However, in his consequence-free environment, even that fails.

He finally finds value in life when he understands that each day is a gift, and he has the opportunity to make a difference with every person he encounters. For about a year I had the words "Remember Groundhog Day" as the screen-saver on my computer, to remind me of the potential that each day holds. I have the ability, through my words and my actions, to significantly alter someone else's experience of today, for good or bad. That's a power each of us has been given by God, and it offers exciting potential to make a difference every day.

I'll end this chapter on a lighter note, just in case you still have doubts about how special you are. At the very, very beginning of your life, when you were still, how shall I say it, very close to your father, you and 300 million of your closest friends lined up for a race. At just the right moment, you all shot forward, and the race was on. This was a unique race in that there could only be one winner, and no prizes for second or third, nor any type of ribbon for just taking part.

Here's the amazing fact: Out of those 300 million sperm (what else did you think I was talking about?!), you won! Out of 300 million competitors, you were the fastest, and you were the one deemed acceptable by your mother's body. Congratulations! Never consider yourself ordinary again!

Truth and a Prayer:

I am special.
I am fearfully and wonderfully made.
I am created in God's image.
He has a purpose for me.

Dear God,
Thank you that I am special to you. Thank you that I bear
your image and that I am fearfully and wonderfully made -
and what's more, I am wanted. Thank you for giving me a
purpose and calling me to make the world a better place today,
through the good deeds You have planned for me to do. Let my
true value in your eyes sink deep into my heart and soul.
In Jesus' Name,
Amen.

Resources

Strobel, Lee   The Case for a Creator
Paperback:
http://www.amazon.com/gp/product/0310242096/ref=a
s_li_ss_tl?ie=UTF8&tag=firstyearinmi-20
Kindle:
http://www.amazon.com/gp/product/B003NX6Y06/ref
=as_li_ss_tl?ie=UTF8&tag=firstyearinmi-20

Denton, Michael   Evolution: A Theory in Crisis
Paperback:
http://www.amazon.com/gp/product/091756152X/ref=
as_li_ss_tl?ie=UTF8&tag=firstyearinmi-20

Hanegraaff, Hank   The Face That Demonstrates
the Farce of Evolution
Paperback:
http://www.amazon.com/gp/product/0849942721/ref=a
s_li_ss_tl?ie=UTF8&tag=firstyearinmi-20
Kindle:
http://www.amazon.com/gp/product/B000W68MPW/re
f=as_li_ss_tl?ie=UTF8&tag=firstyearinmi-20

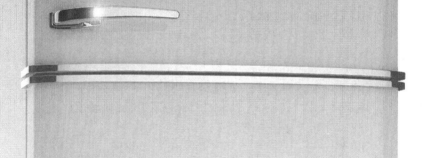

CHAPTER
4

HOW DID MY FAMILY
AFFECT MY SELF-IMAGE?

Robert was 12 years old and living in the children's home where I worked during the summers. He was not having a good morning. He seemed more agitated than usual, and I didn't know why. His level of agitation increased as the morning went on, and finally he became violent toward the other children in the home. I had to restrain him, since he was physically mature for his age and could have done some damage.

When I checked in with the other workers, I found out why his mood was so volatile that morning. Robert's father was due to visit him at the home, and he had a complicated relationship with his father. He loved him, but there was a history of physical and verbal abuse from his father, which had led to Robert being removed from the home for his own safety. This would be a supervised visit, so there would be no risk of abuse in this environment, but still, it stirred up in Robert a maelstrom of emotions that he just did not know how to process.

I finally calmed him down, released him from my grip, took him upstairs, washed his face, and helped him comb his hair so that he could look nice for his dad. As I remember that, my eyes are filling with tears at the tragedy of this child's relationship with his father and what that broken relationship eventually led to.

For many of us, family is a mixed bag. There may be many happy memories, but definitely a few bad ones along with them - or perhaps the mix is tilted heavily in the other direction, with mostly negative experiences and very few good ones to recall.

In terms of how we see ourselves, the way in

which our family reflects "us" back to ourselves is key, since it happens in the most formative years of our life and can leave an almost indelible imprint. A child who is told from a very young age that he is useless and will never amount to anything will find that very hard to shake off. If the people who are supposed to love him the most and who surround him every day give him that sort of feedback, who is he to disagree?

In this chapter, we will consider how fathers, mothers and siblings affect our view of ourselves, and how understanding God as our heavenly Father can radically alter that perspective. I recognize that for some who had brutal or uncaring fathers, the very concept of "father" might be tainted, but my hope and prayer is that as you read, you will see him, and as a result, yourself differently.

Father

I was 29 years old and living in a high-rise apartment in Berlin, Germany. It was my birthday. I was sitting there alone when the phone rang. It was my dad. That in itself was unusual. When I called home, if he answered, he passed me off to my mother as soon as he could. Both he and I knew we didn't have that much to say to each other. However, this time was different. I don't think he had ever initiated a phone call to me before, so even that was surprising, but what he said to me was even more shocking.

"Glyn, I wanted to tell you that I realize I haven't been a very good father to you. I wanted to apologize and ask for your forgiveness."

I didn't know what to say. My throat closed up, and I was near tears. Just a few years earlier that conversation would have been unimaginable. He had had issues with alcohol ever since I remember him joining our family, marrying my mother and adopting me and my brother when I was 5 years old. My memories of Christmas were that it was a dangerous time, when he would probably get drunk at a work party with his scaffolding mates, and then violent, either with some random man at the pub, or toward my mother at home.

When I was a dependent child, he did well enough as a father, but when I grew old enough to question him, and answer back, and disapprove of his behavior, that started the wedge between us. For most of my teenage years, we hardly spoke. He made a few attempts to connect with me, taking me fishing, but I was hopeless at it and would get the lines tangled. We talked about cars and his job, scaffolding, though I would usually lose interest pretty quickly.

One exchange stands out, when I was about to attempt my driving test for the second time. He said to me, "Get it this time," and the reason why that stands out is because it is the only semi-encouraging thing I can remember him saying for almost the whole of my teenage years.

And now this phone call. I think I stammered out that I really appreciated him saying that, and of course, I forgave him. He had become sober through Alcoholics Anonymous and had found faith in a jail cell when he had a vision of hell, and saw Jesus stretching out a hand to him. He took that hand, and never drank again. From that point on he would talk about faith and even tell me that he prayed for me. It was an astonishing transformation and did much to undo the damage of my teenage years.

Many of us have experienced what I shall call a less-than-optimal father. Perhaps your father was like mine, wrapped up in his own issues and addictions, with little warmth and affection directed your way. Perhaps he wasn't around at all, absent physically, having left the family, or absent emotionally, being physically present but uninterested and disengaged. The father's role in the family is to provide strength and stability, and for many of us, that strength was absent or misused, and the stability was nowhere to be seen.

Why that is a problem is this: We are hardwired to receive our father's approval, and if we don't get it, a lack is created in our life. As we saw in chapter 1, that was even necessary for Jesus, and his Father affirmed him at both his baptism and transfiguration. In my case, the lack of approval manifested itself in a desperate desire to receive approval from other sources. I wasn't much to speak of physically in my teenage years, growing only to 5-foot-7 and not being particularly muscular. My chosen sport of table tennis was not one that my dad was really interested in. My avenues for approval became speech and quick thinking. Sure, I might get insulted and abused for my height at school, but you'd better move on quickly, or I would dissect you with a sarcastic remark that made you look about as small as I felt. So I became known for quick thinking, quick sarcastic speech and deadly put-downs.

For many others, the desire to impress a father who is disinterested, or overly critical, has manifested itself in a desperate quest for success in some area, whether that is sports, academics, business or some other pursuit. A drive toward excellence, in that case, is merely a disguised attempt to receive the fatherly approval that has been so lacking.

Particularly for a girl, if the father's attention and approval is absent, that can lead to the pursuit of male attention, healthy or unhealthy, in other environments outside the family, and it often results in promiscuity. When fatherly attention has been lacking, almost any male attention is welcome, and not all males have good intentions, especially in their teenage years, when the hormones seem to drive most of the decision-making. For myself, my goal with my daughter is that she will always feel so utterly loved, cherished, appreciated and affirmed that there is no lack in her. There's no vacuum that leaves her open to those who might not have her best interests at heart.

In religious families poor parenting can take a different twist, with a father who, often conscious of his own drift as a teenager, places tight restrictions on his children. That stifles them in the name of safety, creating a toxic environment in which obedience and perfection are the only true values. There may not be much disobedience in such a household, but there is probably not much laughter or spontaneity either.

One parenting fault to which both parents can fall prey is perfectionism – simply expecting too much from their children. However much the child achieves, however well the child does, the parent always moves the bar just a little bit higher.

"Eight A's and one B – why the heck did you get a B?"

"Second in the class – why aren't you first?"

"97 percent on the test – why did you miss the 3 percent?"

Such attitudes can leave children in despair. They

start to believe that nothing they can ever do is good enough for their parents. However hard they try, however close they come, it still isn't quite enough to achieve the parental approval they crave. When that despair hardens, it turns into resentment against the parent who is impossible to please.

Mother

Lest you think that I am giving fathers a hard time and letting mothers off the hook, let's consider her role. Many of the traits of less-than-optimal fathers can also be experienced by a mother. She can be physically present but emotionally absent.

Perhaps she barely participated in your life, and it felt like practical abandonment. Perhaps your mother suffered from a negative self-image and somehow transferred that to you. Perhaps there was physical or verbal abuse. Perhaps there was a bitterness about unrealized dreams that has permeated your life, too. How many mothers, having failed to become the beauty queen, push their children into child pageants, or other "opportunities" to shine, that actually do not represent anything the child is interested in, but rather a desperate grasping by the mother to validate herself through her child. The pressure on a child to succeed where the parent has failed can be immense.

Statistics show that the number of children being parented by their grandparents rather than their biological parents has increased dramatically over the last few years. That points to physical abandonment, whether voluntary or involuntary, through incarceration, for example.

The mother's role, along with many others, is supposed to be nurturing. She is the soft "other side" to the father's strength, strong in her own way, but with a gentleness, tenderness and protective spirit expressed in the care of her children. She's the one they come running to when they scrape their knees or have a bad day at school. In homes where the mother is not nurturing, that also creates a lack, since her children may not feel secure and experience unconditional love. The old cliché of "Whatever I do, my mother will still love me" may not be true in households where the mother's love is variable and conditional. Some mothers did not grow up in a household where the gentler approach was practiced and were never truly nurtured themselves. It is not surprising that they lack that skill set in their own parenting.

Siblings

Siblings can be another cause of damaged or distorted self-image. In better families, the siblings get along well. There may be a certain amount of argument and rivalry, but it is within healthy boundaries. In dysfunctional families, the rivalry can become toxic or even dangerous.

A biblical example can be found in the story of Joseph, which is recorded in Genesis 37. To summarize, Joseph is favored above the other sons because he is born to his father in his old age. This favoritism is demonstrated in gifts (the coat of many colors) and no doubt a disproportionate share of the father's attention. Joseph has prophetic dreams that show him ruling over everybody else, and he is not shy about sharing those dreams with his brothers.

I think we can clearly establish the evidence for a dysfunctional family here. Jacob the father favors

Joseph over his other children. That is already a recipe for disharmony. Joseph himself is not modest in his retelling of the dreams that predict his future elevation above all other family members, and the other brothers naturally resent him for that, and for being the favorite child, spoiled by the father.

The resentment eventually rises to the level at which they simply do not want Joseph around anymore and will do whatever it takes to get rid of him. They plan to kill him, but then they relent and sell him into slavery instead. The story does eventually have a somewhat happy ending, and there is reconciliation between Joseph and his brothers, but it is a long and difficult road that will get them there.

That was never really a factor in my own upbringing. My brother and I are wired somewhat differently, and so did not tend to compete in the same areas. My parents also seemed happy to let us develop according to our own strengths, and I don't ever remember them saying to either of us, "I wish you were more like your brother."

Perhaps my sisters had a different experience, and maybe it is yours, too. Perhaps you did grow up in the shadow of another sibling, who seemed to do everything better than you and who was "the golden child" in your parents' eyes. Perhaps you were the first child, used to your parents' sole attention, and the arrival of a second one was an unhappy event. I am guessing that for most firstborns that is the case.

A friend of mine who is a pediatrician says that it would be the dynamic equivalent of a husband coming home to his wife and telling her he is bringing another wife into the house. "I'm not saying there's anything wrong with you as a wife, but I just feel the need to add another." We can understand the reaction that would get, and that's somewhat close to the emotional reaction of a firstborn who for the first time has to share the attention of his or her parents with this newcomer who seems particularly demanding and needy.

If children feel that they can never live up to the performance of another sibling, that can lead to a deeply held perception of being "second best," not quite making the grade, a bit of a disappointment really. That forms a self-image issue of being "not quite good enough" that can be hard to shake.

Abuse

Now we come to the tricky and tragic subject of abuse. It is tricky because it may bring up painful memories that have been dormant for years, and tragic because the family should be the safe haven, where we are known and loved for who we are, where we feel secure. When that environment is not a safe haven, serious damage can be done to our self-image.

It hardly needs explaining that children who suffer physical abuse will think that they are unloved and unwanted. Children who are sexually abused will receive a distorted perception of love and physical touch. Children who are verbally abused will find it hard to believe anything good about themselves. Such childhood imprints go deep.

A child who is the victim of divorce (not that divorce is intentional abuse) will often feel partly to blame for the breakup of the parents' marriage. Of course, a child in a household in which the parents are constantly at war with each other will not feel secure either.

The reason why that is so damaging to children, and to the adults they will become, is rooted in child psychology. A child finds it very hard to believe that his or her parents are evil, or doing wrong. In order to make sense out of the abuse they receive, children draw the understandable conclusion that they must deserve it, that there is something about them that means they should be abused. It is all too easy for a boy or girl to reach the understanding that the divorce is happening "because I am a bad girl" or because "I am a bad boy."

As tragic as that is, it is not beyond repair. It is not beyond the reach of our loving God, who can restore to us the image and self-worth that have been compromised through such negative treatment.

God as Father

Let's consider God as Father and see how he compares to the earthly fathers we have experienced.

As we said in chapter 2, before Jesus ever did any ministry, God the Father affirmed his love and approval of him. It was not a performance-based response, but rather the declaration of love and affirmation comes just because Jesus is God's Son. There's no standard he has to reach, no achievement or success he has to accomplish. The affirmation and love come just from the basis of relationship, not performance. In the same way, the heavenly Father's love for us is not based on performance. It is based on the simple fact that we are his children, and we belong to him:

> *12 Yet to all who received him, to those who believed in his name, he gave the right to become children of God - 13*

children born not of natural descent, nor of human decision or a husband's will, but born of God. (John 1:12-13)

In fact, our ability to influence God's love and acceptance of us, including the very issue of salvation, is quashed by the apostle Paul in his letter to the Roman church:

6 you see, at just the right time, when we were still powerless, Christ died for the ungodly. 7 Very rarely will anyone die for a righteous man, though for a good man someone might possibly dare to die. 8 But God demonstrates his own love for us in this: While we were still sinners, Christ died for us. (Romans 5:8)

What that passage makes clear is that we have nothing to contribute to our own salvation. It was "while we were still sinners" that Christ died for us. At the point in time that Paul references, he had not had his experience on the Damascus Road. In fact, he was actively engaged in seeking out and persecuting Christians. That's not an impressive record for someone seeking to get into God's good books. But what Paul realized was this: that God loved him, even when he was dead-set on killing off this new group called Christians.

In our own experience, we realize that Christ's decision to die for our sins happened even before we were born. The all-knowing God knew the life we would lead and still allowed his Son to take our place. There is nothing of our own merit and goodness in the equation. It is purely and simply the love of God. For me, that is a liberating truth, because if my salvation depended on me, I would be forever anxious that I would somehow fail in my performance and lose it in some way. This verse in Romans makes it abundantly clear that it is God's love that secures my salvation, not my performance.

There is another wonderful passage about God as a father in Hosea 11, where God speaks about his relationship to his people as using father/son imagery:

> *1 "When Israel was a child, I loved him,*
> *and out of Egypt I called my son.*
> *2 But the more I called Israel,*
> *the further they went from me.*
> *They sacrificed to the Baals*
> *and they burned incense to images.*
> *3 It was I who taught Ephraim to walk,*
> *taking them by the arms;*
> *but they did not realize*
> *it was I who healed them.*
> *4 I led them with cords of human kindness,*
> *with ties of love;*
> *I lifted the yoke from their neck*
> *and bent down to feed them.*

See the key points here: he loved Israel because he was his son. He recalls how that taught Israel (Ephraim) to walk, taking them by the arms. Any parent reading this will probably recall the happy days when you held your children's arms as they placed their small feet on your big feet and "walked" with you. Despite the frequent rebellion of this people, and their disobedience, the tenderness is still apparent. God says that he "healed them [and] led them with cords of human kindness [and] bent down to feed them." Those are expressions of tender, fatherly gentleness, suffused with an unconditional love.

Later in the chapter, though, God would have every reason to abandon them because of their continued sin, rebellion and worship of idols, but he refuses to do so, saying:

> 8 *"How can I give you up, Ephraim?*
> *How can I hand you over, Israel?*
> *How can I treat you like Admah?*
> *How can I make you like Zeboiim?*
> *My heart is changed within me;*
> *all my compassion is aroused.*

God cannot give them up; he cannot abandon them. His love is too strong, his compassion too great.

How many of us have longed for a father like that – steeped in unconditional love, tender and strong at the same time, protective and even nurturing? That is the father we find in God the heavenly Father. We do not need to impress him. We do not need to promote or justify ourselves. We just need to relax into his love. We need to understand that there is nothing we can do that would cause God to love us more or love us less. He loves us because we are his children. That is it. That is about as complicated as it gets.

In the person of Jesus, God-come-in-the-flesh, we also find nurturing aspects. When he approached Jerusalem, desiring more than anything else to lead the people back to the God who loved them, this is how he expressed it:

> *"O Jerusalem, Jerusalem, you who kill the prophets and*
> *stone those sent to you, how often I have longed to gather*

your children together, as a hen gathers her chicks under her wings, but you were not willing! (Matthew 23:37)

That is actually a very feminine image of nurture and protection, with the language similar to how a hen might protect her chicks from a fire or a predator. In God we find both the traits that are normally more associated with the masculine and the nurturing, protective instincts more often attributed to the feminine. In God we find the perfect Father, who in himself also carries the qualities of a perfect mother. It is in his strength, his love and his care that we can finally find rest.

A note to parents:

As I've discussed parenting in this chapter, you may have identified some areas in which your own parenting falls short. Take heart. Chapter 6 will provide some encouragement. In the meantime, perhaps read through again and study the attributes that make God the perfect parent, and think about how you can express those in a meaningful way to your children. For example, whenever my son achieves an award (for school or taekwondo), I tell him how proud I am of him, but then say something like, "Do you know what I am even more proud of? Just that you are my son." In that way, I hope to accentuate the truth that my love and approval of him are not based on performance or awards, but simply because he is my son and I am his father. I take random moments just to tell my son and daughter, "Do you know something? I am so happy to be your daddy. I am so proud that you are my little boy" or "girl."

I think that as I do that, I am communicating the

unconditional love that the Father in heaven has for each of us. As that sinks deep into their hearts and minds, I want them to know that no failure, no mistake, no bad choice will ever threaten the love I have for them. I want them to sense that the love I have for them is unassailable, and that they can find their security and sense of worth in that.

Truth and a Prayer

I am not my family.
I am loved by a heavenly Father with an unbreakable love.
I am his, and he is mine.

Dear God, my Father in heaven,
Thank you for loving me with an unbreakable love. There is nothing I can do to make you love me more; there is nothing I can do to make you love me less. All that I am I bring to you, confident in your love and acceptance of me. Thank you that my performance, my failures and even my successes are unimportant to you. You love me simply because I am your child. Help me rest in that truth.
In Jesus' Name,
Amen.

Resources

Wright, Dr. H. Norman A Dad-Shaped Hole in My heart
http://www.amazon.com/gp/product/0764200747/ref=as_li_ss_tl?ie=UTF8&camp=1789 &creative=390957&creativeASIN=0764200747&link Code=as2&tag=firstyearinmi-20

Jarema, William J.   There's a Hole in My Chest: healing and Hope for Adult Children Everywhere
http://www.amazon.com/gp/product/0824515722/ref=as_li_ss_tl?ie=UTF8&tag=firstye arinmi-20

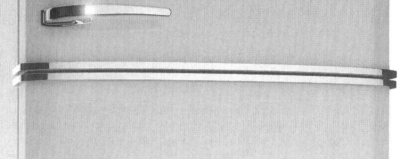

CHAPTER

5

WHO DOES SOCIETY SAY I AM?

When I was 8 or 9 years old, the most popular playground game in my school was called "Top Trumps." Top Trumps was a card game, and each pack of cards represented a certain group of items, such as "Ships" or "Aircraft." There was a list of numerical data on each individual card. The goal of the game was to get all the other cards, and the way you won cards was that a player would select a category and read out the statistic for that category, and then the other players would read theirs. The one with the best statistic would win.

In the case of cars, for example, "Top Speed" would be a category, and the person with the Ferrari or Lamborghini would choose that as the statistic. If you were holding the card representing the Mini, since it had a lower top speed, you would hand your card over to the player with the highest.

The one I remember best was the "Ships" game. If you were holding the American aircraft carrier card, and it was your turn, you would choose "Displacement" as your category and be guaranteed to win that round, since nothing else came close to how much water an American aircraft carrier could displace. If you held the pursuit boat, you would choose "Top Speed," because 55 knots was pretty much unbeatable by any other craft at that time.

The quirk of the game is that each player, on his turn, could decide what the standard of measurement would be. You could be holding the aircraft carrier card, but it might not be your turn, and though you would dearly love the standard to be "Displacement," the other player might call "Top Speed," and you would lose the card.

It occurs to me that much of our lives is lived the

same way. Someone somewhere has decided that this certain thing – wealth or fame, for example – is the measure of true success and value. Whether we really wanted to or not, we have gone along with that measurement , and we rate ourselves and others according to it. The question this chapter seeks to answer is: Who really sets the standard, and what really is an accurate measure of our value?

The danger is that we will adopt the same value system as society, and unless we match the standards by which value is normally ascribed, we will consider ourselves substandard and lacking in worth. Society says we are valuable if we:

a) have impressive personal wealth;
b) are famous, (or fame's inferior cousin, a celebrity); or
c) have exceptional talent.

But what are we left with, if we have none of those things? Playing the lottery, and living vicarious lives through TV shows ("MTV Cribs," for example) that depict the lavish lifestyles of the rich and famous? Surely God has something more than that for us. He does. Read on.

I am worth my currency value

By far the most common standard of measurement is wealth. If you took a random poll and asked people to name someone who is successful, the high probability is that they will name someone who is extremely wealthy. It could be a successful businessperson such as Bill Gates (net worth, $66 billion in September 2012) or Warren Buffett ($46 billion).

Others may be renowned for their talent or

ingenuity, but with that comes the reward that society places on such talent, and if you look beneath the surface, the talent usually assists someone, or some company, in making a lot of money. Mark Zuckerberg, founder of Facebook, has a personal net worth of $9.4 billion, but it is the potential of profits through social networking that has the shareholders excited.

Sports stars also rank very highly on this measure. Evan Longoria, baseball player with the Tampa Bay Rays, agreed on November 27, 2012, to a $136.6-million, 10-year contract. Such a huge amount is not because of the inherent generosity of the team's owners but surely reflects confidence that having such a popular and successful player on board will be good for ticket sales, shirt sales, and who knows what other merchandise that will be attached to his name. In the end, profit potential is reflected in the package offered.

Those in the entertainment industry would also qualify highly on this measure. Music companies and movie companies do not pay a star or fund a film out of the kindness of their hearts, or even (I suspect) in response to the raw talent of the performer. Rather, the amount paid reflects the belief that through marketing this music or movie, there is profit to be had. So, stars such as Justin Bieber (net worth, $110 million) and Lady Gaga ($150 million) are revered not just for their "talent" but for their marketability.

The revealing factor in all of the above is found in the simple phrase "net worth." In each of those examples, I noted their net worth in the most common form in which it is expressed: dollars. However, who decided that the amount of currency we possess is the category on the card of life that we should use? Who decided that dollars is the right way to calculate somebody's value? The ironic thing is that probably 98 percent of us would not even question whether the people listed so far are successful. In fact, from the little information I have provided, all you know is what purchasing power they have. That is, in reality, such a thin slice of the whole, and an inadequate measure of a person.

What if I added other categories and used them as a measurement. What if I added:

- has a healthy relationship with parents
- has a positive self-image
- has a happy marriage or significant other relationship
- sleeps well at night and is not anxious
- has a clear conscience
- has a low stress level
- is in good physical health
- has a strong, supportive circle of true friends
- has a good relationship with his or her children ...

... and so on. If we saw a person stepping out of a Rolls Royce at the airport, into a personal Lear jet, we would automatically consider that person to be successful – but by what measure? Perhaps the person is dying of cancer and has only three weeks to live. Perhaps the individual just went through a bitter divorce and is estranged from his kids. Perhaps the person has a serious drug problem, using narcotics to dull the deep, emotional pain he or she feels from the ways all the money has been earned and people have been exploited. We know none of that, simply from observing what the individual possesses in terms of material wealth.

In the New Testament, we see Jesus encounter the rich on a number of occasions, and usually he doesn't seem that impressed. As a sample, let's take the story in which he meets the "rich young ruler":

18 A certain ruler asked him, "Good teacher, what must I do to inherit eternal life?"

19 "Why do you call me good?" Jesus answered. "No one is good-except God alone. 20 You know the commandments: 'Do not commit adultery, do not murder, do not steal, do not give false testimony, honor your father and mother.'"

21 "All these I have kept since I was a boy," he said.

22 When Jesus heard this, he said to him, "You still lack one thing. Sell everything you have and give to the poor, and you will have treasure in heaven. Then come, follow me."

23 When he heard this, he became very sad, because he was a man of great wealth. 24 Jesus looked at him and said, "How hard it is for the rich to enter the kingdom of God! 25 Indeed, it is easier for a camel to go through the eye of a needle than for a rich man to enter the kingdom of God."

26 Those who heard this asked, "Who then can be saved?"

27 Jesus replied, "What is impossible with men is possible with God."

28 Peter said to him, "We have left all we had to follow you!"

29 "I tell you the truth," Jesus said to them, "no one who has left home or wife or brothers or parents or children for the sake of the kingdom of God will fail to receive many times as much in this age and, in the age to come, eternal life." (Luke 18:18-30)

This is a very interesting encounter. You would think that Jesus would be positively disposed toward someone who is publicly interested in following him and who seems to be making a genuine inquiry about the nature of true discipleship. Yet Jesus, after assessing a few preliminaries, hones in on the one factor that, for this man, will be the deal-breaker: his personal wealth. It seems to me that this man is reading from the wrong category. His assessment of his own value is largely connected to his wealth, and unless Jesus can break him of that, the man will never be able to understand what really counts. Jesus understands that, and reaffirms that it is hard for the rich to enter the Kingdom of God. Why? Because they are tempted to trust in their own wealth rather than trust in God, and that is a barrier to be overcome. Like all of us, they must learn to assess by different categories. Wealth, rather than being an advantage in the Kingdom of God, is a potential liability.

Even those in professional Christian ministry can fall for that temptation. In the New Testament, James tells the churches not to give preferential treatment to the rich:

My brothers, as believers in our glorious Lord Jesus Christ, don't show favoritism. 2 Suppose a man comes into your meeting wearing a gold ring and fine clothes, and a poor man in shabby clothes also comes in. 3 If you show special attention to the man wearing fine clothes and say, "Here's a good seat for you," but say to the poor man, "You stand there" or "Sit on the floor by my feet," 4 have you not discriminated among yourselves and become judges with evil thoughts? (James 2:1-4)

In our 21st-century context, most pastors would be much more inviting than Jesus if a rich person expressed a desire to join their church, justifying their enthusiasm with thoughts of an increased "tithe" that would enable them to accomplish more of the Lord's work. Even those, who more than most should be in agreement with the value system of Jesus, are easily swayed and impressed by worldly wealth, and will be tempted to give those people preference of opinion in the way church affairs are managed. I admire pastors who can remain true to their convictions, even when a decision they make might mean the departure of generous contributors from the church.

The assessment of value expressed through currency also is reflected in salaries. It is telling what a society rewards. Let me give you an example of a few professions, and their average salary, in the United States, 2012 (data from Payscale.com and Salary.com):

Elementary School Teacher	$40,223
High School Teacher	$43, 954
Certified Nursing Assistant	$33,610
Paramedic	$38,583
Investment Banker	$121, 690
Private Banker	$116,560

Obviously, I am cherry-picking my examples here to make a point, (and honestly, I have no gripe against those in the financial professions), but even so, it is obvious that we place a very high value (in terms of the level of reward) on those who create or increase wealth, while those who shape our children's minds, keep us alive after a severe car accident and tend our wounds as we recover are paid much less. What does that say about our value system?

The three underlying problems with this value system are: 1) It is not necessarily one that is acknowledged by the most important and objective authority in the universe, God himself; 2) It is extremely vulnerable to a change in circumstances, and 3) An increase in wealth is no guarantee of happiness or improved self-image

When you scan the Bible for what it is that God sees as praiseworthy, you rarely find any mention of material wealth. Instead, what God deems worthy is character: patience, kindness, compassion and self-control. When material wealth is mentioned, it is usually accompanied by instructions on how to use such wealth wisely, to take care of the poor, the foreigner and the widow in their midst – which begs the question, why would we want to base our self-image and sense of value, on something that God seems so unimpressed by? In fact, even by our own standards, individuals we would think of as admirable, such as Mother Theresa, had very little in the way of personal wealth but were exemplary in character.

The Bible also addresses the second issue, namely, the variability of wealth:

> *Command those who are rich in this present world not to be arrogant nor to put their hope in wealth, which is so uncertain, but to put their hope in God, who richly provides us with everything for our enjoyment. (1 Timothy 6:17)*

Putting your trust in wealth, and building your self-image on your accumulation of material possessions and money is a house of cards, and it can easily come crashing down. The periodic financial crises we experience serve as useful reminders that this is a shaky foundation on which to base your sense of self.

Lastly, though The Beatles told us that "money can't buy me love," many of us suspect that it will serve as an acceptable substitute. We believe that we will be happier if we are wealthier, and so we spend our time and energy in the pursuit of greater income.

You might be surprised to learn that lottery winners, who experience a sudden increase in wealth, are not happier long-term as a result. This extract is from www.theatlantic.com:

"In a well-known 1978 study from Northwestern University, researchers surveyed a small group of major lottery winners, paralyzed accident victims, and a control group. They found two surprising things about lottery winners. Not only were they not happier than the controls, but also they 'took significantly less pleasure from a series of mundane events,' which is rather unfortunate, considering that most of life consists of a series of non-extraordinary events.

"Crucially, it was determined that the lottery winners' blasé attitude was not due to 'preexisting differences between people who buy or do not buy lottery tickets,' suggesting that the lottery victory itself changed their perspective.

"What's going on? It's all about the psychological power of adaptation and relativity with money. Adaptation: At first, the thrill of becoming millions of dollars richer is, well thrilling, but after a while, the thrill wears off. Relativity: Winning the lottery creates an indelible memory, a comparison point that makes typical life events seem disappointing and boring. Money can buy happiness, if you know how to spend it, but the incidence of winning the lottery does not, on its own, buy much happiness at all. In the long-term, it can be a net cost to life satisfaction." (http://www.theatlantic.com/business/archive/2012/11/the-economic-case-against-winning-a-500-million-lottery-seriously/265709/)

The lesson is clear: Don't build your self-image on wealth. Don't build it on how society evaluates you, by the arbitrary standards of wealth, fame, celebrity or exceptional talent. Those can all be fleeting and uncertain, and they are a shaky foundation for forming a true view of who we are and what we are worth.

The sum of my achievements

Talent is another quality that is highly prized by society, and often financially rewarded, at least in the sporting arena (starving artists and musicians might beg to differ!). The problem with basing your self-image on your talent is its variability.

In the old westerns on TV, the young, hotshot, quick-on-the-draw gunslinger was always looking over his shoulder, afraid of who was going to try and take him on, beat him, and thus establish his own reputation. The stress of being the best, or better than almost everybody else, can damage a person. Rather than seeing others as colleagues, they become competitors. Rather than enjoying the talents and success of others, we can become envious and jealous – neither of which is a particularly attractive character trait.

I remember hearing a rabbinic story told by noted author David Augsburger, who has written extensively on forgiveness. He tells of a tailor who for years had been the most accomplished and talented tailor in the town. All the people used to come to him for their fine clothes, and he had even made garments for the king. He enjoyed this success for decades, but then started to reach older age, and noticed that his stitching was not quite so fine, his eyesight not quite as sharp. Still, he had an established reputation, so his business continued to flourish, and if anybody noticed the slight decrease in quality, nobody mentioned it to him.

Then a new tailor came to the town – young, keen, with perfect eyesight and exceptional talent. Before long, he was the talk of the town, and bit by bit, the business started migrating toward him. The old tailor could do nothing to stop it and really could not rival the skill of the young pretender. In his bitterness and desperation, he cried out to the Lord for relief, for some solution to this distress.

The Lord heard his prayer and that night, he sent an angel to the old tailor. The angel woke him from his restless sleep and said this to him: "The Lord has instructed me to grant you a wish. But whatever you wish for, you should know that he will give the young tailor a double portion of what you receive."

The old man thought, and then a sly and wicked grin came over his face. He looked up at the angel and said: "I have considered my wish. I wish you to make me blind in one eye!"

When we base our self-image on our exceptional talent, we are prone to just such attitudes, despising others for their success because they challenge our illusion of uniqueness. If they can do something as well as, or better than, we can, then suddenly we have lost our sense of being special.

Most talents, over time, will peak and then diminish. There are few talents that continue to advance the older we get. I recently took a belt-promotion test for taekwondo, and it was very different from the martial arts tests I did in my 20s. For some reason, I am slower, and my body definitely requires longer recovery time after such an arduous experience. Physical prowess and sporting ability will diminish. Beauty will fade. A sharp mind will eventually become less sharp. Talent is a double-edged sword. While we have it, and while it is impressive and superior, it can sustain and thrill us. When it is gone or diminished, however, the sword can cut us. It's a shaky basis on which to shape our self-image.

There's a Bible story which demonstrates this, relating to Saul's reputation as a warrior:

> *5 Whatever Saul sent him to do, David did it so successfully that Saul gave him a high rank in the army. This pleased all the people, and Saul's officers as well.*

> *6 When the men were returning home after David had killed the Philistine, the women came out from all the towns of Israel to meet King Saul with singing and dancing, with joyful songs and with tambourines and lutes. 7 As they danced, they sang:*

> *"Saul has slain his thousands,*
> *and David his tens of thousands."*
> *8 Saul was very angry; this refrain galled him. "They have credited David with tens of thousands," he thought, "but me with only thousands. What more can he get but the kingdom?" 9 And from that time on Saul kept a jealous eye on David. (1 Samuel 18:5-8)*

We can see it clearly here. Saul's high view of himself was based on the reputation he had as the most superior warrior in all of Israel, but now, David, his protégé, had gained an even better reputation, and Saul burned with jealousy, to the point that he tried to eliminate his rival by killing him.

Where this performance-based perspective gets tricky is when our view of ourselves is mixed in with how we live out our faith. In this paragraph, I'm going to assume that my readers are Christians and generally seek to please God by how they live, and that "society" in this context refers to the smaller category of "church society" and the opinions of other Christians. Seeking to please God with the way we lead our life is all well and good, up to the point that we start to think our performance as Christians makes any difference at all in how much God loves us. The danger is that we begin to rate ourselves, and thus form self-image, on the basis of how well we think we are "doing" at Christianity.

When we do that, we are falling into the same trap as the Galatian church in the Bible. Many of them had formerly been committed Jews, and as such, they were used to viewing religion as a matter of following the rules. That was never supposed to be the focus. The original purpose of the Law (10 commandments, etc.) was to reveal the character of God to his people, and it was received with delight (see Psalm 119, for example), but over time, the focus became the Law itself, rather than the God behind the Law.

When the Jews in the Galatian church became Christians, they experienced a wonderful freedom as they understood that the basis of their acceptance by

God was no longer obedience to the Law, but the sacrifice of Christ on the cross. However, a group known as Judaizers infiltrated the Galatian church and distorted the gospel to such an extent that the apostle Paul had to write a scathing letter to the Galatian Christians, telling them that they were abandoning the true gospel. The message of the Judaizers was that, yes, it is fine to accept and follow Jesus Christ, but you must also be keeping the Jewish Law.

The reason Paul was so upset was that it implied that acceptance by God was once again viewed as a matter of performance rather than as a gift of grace through the action of Christ on the cross. Similarly, when we start to build our self-image on the basis of our religious performance, we can easily fall into the traps of pride, comparison and judgmentalism.

We are in danger of pride, because now we think that we are contributing something to our own salvation (this belief, promoted by Pelagius in the early centuries of the Christian church, was condemned as a heresy). We are in danger of comparison, because once we start focusing on our performance, we will begin looking around us to see how well others are doing by these standards, and either we will think we are doing better – at which point pride and judgmentalism will again enter in – or we may believe that we are doing worse, and become depressed or competitive. It becomes evident that those perspectives are not in line with the gospel, and like other performance-based building blocks of self-image, they are subject to variability. Our "performance" as Christians will vary. Sometimes we will be very obedient and in tune with the purposes of God. Sometimes we will not - but that does not affect our acceptance by God. Ephesians 2:8-9 states:

> *For it is by grace you have been saved, through faith - and this not from yourselves, it is the gift of God - not by works, so that no one can boast.*

"Not from yourselves" – it is, in the end, not down to us, and if God does not view or accept us on the basis of our performance, what right have we to do it? Do we know better than God? Do we wish to rival the gift of Christ on the cross with our own contribution? Do we think we can supplement it? Put that way, I hope it sounds as ridiculous to you as it does to me.

We are saved not through our performance, our obedience, our achievements or any other contribution that we could make. We are saved by grace. We are saved by the unmerited favor of God. Salvation is a gift, and our only part is to open up our hands to receive it. Naturally, genuine salvation will result in a life that aims to please God, but that is the response to salvation, not the means of achieving it.

I realize that concentrating on the church, and how we view ourselves as part of the "society" of the church or Christians, is not "wider society," but for those of us who are Christians, it forms a dominant part of our social circle. We can easily be influenced by the way others in the church view us. Though we may think that being viewed as a "super saint" is a positive boost to our self-image, it is not. It moves us toward a performance-based view of ourselves, which is subject to variability and the ever-changing opinions of others, rather than the settled and consistent view of us that God himself holds.

Why do we love children, who are not productive, and have neither wealth or talent?

Let's consider the question of why we love children, particularly babies. In their new form, they are totally dependent on others for their well-being. They cannot sit up, they cannot feed themselves, they cannot go to the bathroom in an appropriate environment. They are poor conversationalists, restricting themselves to a few gurgles and crying. They do not tell you what is wrong when they are upset, and you have to go through a sequence of guesses (hungry, tired, thirsty, diaper full of poop, gas?) until you find the one that seems to make a difference. They are very unproductive members of the family. They never do any chores or help around the house. They are, to be honest, very unproductive members of society. They invent nothing and produce nothing worthwhile. In fact, they are little more than food processing machines taking in milk or formula at one end, and producing something like a combination of Velcro and nuclear waste at the other, which poor parents have to deal with, usually without the protection of a hazmat suit.

Really, on the basis of their performance and contribution, they are worth very little – and that"s precisely the point. Performance and contribution are the wrong measures for the value of a baby. Parents love babies simply because they belong to them. Others love babies because our natural instinct is to care for and protect the vulnerable, and those who are not kind to babies are viewed, quite rightly, with some suspicion.

In the same way, performance and contribution are

the wrong measures for *our* value. Our value consists primarily not in who we are (in terms of wealth, fame, talent), but *whose* we are, God's dearly loved children, accepted simply because we belong to him.

I am more than a victim of circumstances, a product of my environment

Let's consider the biblical story of someone who would have been viewed as of little value by society, but who in the end is reminded about her true value in the eyes of God. The story is found in Mark, chapter 5:

> *A large crowd followed and pressed around him. 25 And a woman was there who had been subject to bleeding for twelve years. 26 She had suffered a great deal under the care of many doctors and had spent all she had, yet instead of getting better she grew worse. 27 When she heard about Jesus, she came up behind him in the crowd and touched his cloak, 28 because she thought, "If I just touch his clothes, I will be healed." 29 Immediately her bleeding stopped and she felt in her body that she was freed from her suffering.*

> *30 At once Jesus realized that power had gone out from him. He turned around in the crowd and asked, "Who touched my clothes?"*

> *31 "You see the people crowding against you," his disciples answered, "and yet you can ask, 'Who touched me?' "*

> *32 But Jesus kept looking around to see who had done it. 33 Then the woman, knowing what had happened to her, came and fell at his feet and, trembling with fear, told him the whole truth. 34 he said to her, "Daughter, your faith has healed you. Go in peace and be freed from your suffering." (Mark 5:24b-33)*

Let's think about this. The Jews had very particular rules about blood, and the fact that the woman has been bleeding for 12 years meant that she was pretty much cut off from the religious and spiritual life of the community, since you couldn't go to the synagogue if you were bleeding. Even if you sat on a piece of furniture in that condition, the furniture would have been tainted by your "uncleanness." Not only that, but in Judaic society, sickness was often viewed as a punishment from God for sin – see the story of the man born blind in John 9 as an example – so the community would have thought that she was somehow responsible, somehow deficient in her walk with God. That would have created both religious and social isolation: if she touched anyone during her time of bleeding, those people would become ritually unclean. It's easy to understand how disconnected this woman would feel, having such a problem and being excluded from so much of village life.

I think we can fairly conclude that this woman had a physical problem, a spiritual problem, a social and relational problem and an emotional problem. She probably wouldn't dare approach Jesus directly – it would be a bad thing to make a rabbi ritually unclean – so she sneaked in behind him, and with great faith touched his garment, figuring that even touching his clothes might work to heal her. And she was right – it did. Jesus was sensitive to the fact that power had gone out from him, and the woman revealed herself as the one responsible. The text says, "She told him the whole truth."

From the perspective of society, she was unclean and viewed as an outcast, feeling spiritually disconnected and socially removed. Now, she was the center of attention, her healing was confirmed, and more than that, Jesus praised her faith. She was now physically well, it has been announced to the community, her social and religious isolation are at an end. The rabbi did not rebuke her for her audacity but instead praised her for her faith, thereby declaring to her and everyone listening that there was nothing wrong with her spiritually.

In effect, Jesus announced to the people around her that the most important thing about her was that she was a daughter with great faith. In the end, it is what he said about her that was defining, not how she was viewed by society.

The same is true for us. In the eyes of society, we may not be wealthy, we may not be famous, we may not be exceptionally talented – but those things are unimportant. It is what Jesus says about us that actually counts - and counts for all eternity. To those of us who have faith, who have trusted in him, he calls us "son" and "daughter." We belong to him, and in the end, that's the only thing that matters. Society is shallow. Fashion is fickle. The Word of the Lord, what Jesus says, lasts forever.

Truth and a Prayer

I am not who society says I am.
I am not the sum of my wealth, my fame or my talents.
I am who God says I am.

Lord God,
Thank you that your love for me is not based on the variable elements of money, fame or talent. You love me not for how I perform, but for who I am: your child. Thank you that this love does not waver or falter but remains strong and consistent, never changing. Let me feel that love today, and let it inoculate me against the siren songs of the other voices.
In Jesus Name,
Amen.

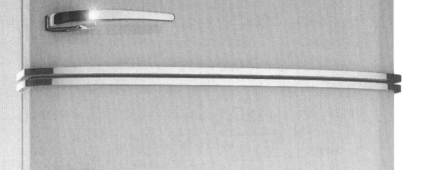

CHAPTER

6

SINNED AGAINST: WHAT HAVE THEY DONE TO ME?

You can't use Kirk

He was 15 years old, skinny and insecure. Somehow Kirk mustered up the courage to try out for the junior varsity football team, though he knew the odds of getting playing time were slim. The situation wasn't helped by a coach who seemed to take a personal dislike to him and used him as a knock-down tackle dummy for a bigger kid, leaving him in a heap on the ground as they walked away uncaring.

For most of the football season he did little more than dress out and sit on the bench watching others play football. Then one day, his big chance came. There was an injury to one of the players on the field, so one of the coaches came up to him and said the magic words, "Kirk, get in there." With tremendous excitement he strapped on his helmet and started to run out on the field when a hand reached out, caught the back of his shoulder pads at his neck, yanked him back and said, "No, can't use Kirk." It was the same coach who had told that kid during practice to hit him hard enough to knock the wind out of him.

"Can't use Kirk." Those tormenting words played over and over in his mind for years.

The hurtful words, and painful actions of others, can have repercussions that last years, creating a seemingly indelible stamp on our self-image. It doesn't take much, especially in our formative years, to convince us that our worst fears are true – that we aren't attractive, that we do not have any special skills, that we will not amount to anything, that we are a waste of space, unwanted and un-liked. In a strange twist of psychology, we seem much more ready to believe the bad about ourselves than the good, and the damage done by hurtful words and actions is disproportionate. Estimates state that it takes somewhere between 10 and 37 positive comments to offset the damage that one negative one can cause.

Our ability to take such input and turn it into a major source of our self-image is tragic. It is a small step from hearing such comments to defining ourselves by the negativity. The label becomes the identity. So I am no longer a person who occasionally struggles with too much alcohol consumption ... I am an alcoholic. I am not a person who fails from time to time ... I am a failure. I am not a person who, because of economic circumstances, is out of a job right now ... I am a loser. I am no longer just a person who flirts with drug abuse ... I am an addict. I am no longer someone who has to sell my body to make enough money to feed my children ... I am a prostitute, and what I have to do becomes the core of my identity - which brings us neatly to a Bible story featuring just such a character.

The scene is a semi-public dinner party at Simon the Pharisee's house, and this is how it plays out ...

36 Now one of the Pharisees invited Jesus to have dinner with him, so he went to the Pharisee's house and reclined at the table. 37 When a woman who had lived a sinful life in that town learned that Jesus was eating at the Pharisee's house, she brought an alabaster jar of perfume, 38 and as she stood behind him at his feet weeping, she began to wet his feet with her tears. Then she wiped them with her hair, kissed them and poured perfume on them.

39 When the Pharisee who had invited him saw this, he said to himself, "If this man were a prophet, he would know who is touching him and what kind of woman she is - that she is a sinner."

40 Jesus answered him, "Simon, I have something to tell you."

"Tell me, teacher," he said.

41 "Two men owed money to a certain moneylender. One owed him five hundred denarii, and the other fifty. 42 Neither of them had the money to pay him back, so he canceled the debts of both. Now which of them will love him more?"

43 Simon replied, "I suppose the one who had the bigger debt canceled."

"You have judged correctly," Jesus said.

44 Then he turned toward the woman and said to Simon, "Do you see this woman? I came into your house. You did not give me any water for my feet, but she wet my feet with her tears and wiped them with her hair. 45 you did not give me a kiss, but this woman, from the time I entered, has not stopped kissing my feet. 46 you did not put oil on my head, but she has poured perfume on my feet. 47 Therefore, I tell you, her many sins have been forgiven - for she loved much. But he who has been forgiven little loves little."

48 Then Jesus said to her, "Your sins are forgiven."

49 The other guests began to say among themselves, "Who is this who even forgives sins?"

50 Jesus said to the woman, "Your faith has saved you; go in peace." (Luke 7:36-50)

This whole scene is rich with theological importance, and thanks to an excellent work of Kenneth Bailey, in *Poet and Peasant and Through Peasant Eyes*, we are able to grasp most of it. The text is somewhat euphemistic in saying that the woman had led a sinful life. Everyone reading it in its original context, and for sure the people at the dinner party, would have known the type of woman she was: a prostitute.

She becomes overwhelmed at the sight of Jesus, wets his feet with her tears, dries them with her hair, and then pours perfume on them. Her response to Jesus is in marked contrast to that of Simon, who has failed as a host. He did not wash and dry Jesus' feet, or have one of his servants do so. He did not greet Jesus with the kiss normally given to an acknowledged teacher or rabbi. He did not anoint him with oil.

And then Jesus does a number of things that are completely taboo in that society. First, he talks about the woman, when the consensus of the time was that women should not be mentioned in public. That taboo went so far that a Jewish man traveling on business, who had only his wife and daughters at home, would not address a letter to them, but to the son he one day hoped to father! Such are the extreme measures a Jewish man would go to in order to avoid mentioning women in public.

There is a beautiful irony in verse 39:

> *39 When the Pharisee who had invited him saw this, he said to himself, "If this man were a prophet, he would know who is touching him and what kind of woman she is - that she is a sinner."*

The irony is this: Simon fails to acknowledge that Jesus is a true prophet, but Jesus is a true prophet, and that reveals that Simon's perception of him is very flawed. Second, he thinks Jesus doesn't know who is touching him, but Jesus does. Third, Simon thinks he knows what kind of woman she is, but he doesn't. He knows what kind of woman she was and identifies her as (still) a sinner. However, Jesus sees her as she truly is, a forgiven sinner, and that makes all the difference. Fourth, Simon thinks there is a sinner in the room whose very presence defiles, and Jesus agrees with him - but from Jesus' perspective, Simon is the judgmental, merciless Pharisee who cannot understand or perceive a transformed life, and he is the sinner who defiles, as Jesus makes clear in the following verses.

One of the major theological points of the story is that the woman was forgiven, for she loved much. The original Greek translation makes it clear that it was not her action that achieved forgiveness from Jesus. Rather, it was her overwhelming gratitude at already having been forgiven that elicited her response to Jesus. Her "loving much" was a response to forgiveness and salvation, not a drastic attempt to earn it.

Someone once said that Jesus never met a prostitute. Before those around could grab their Bibles and prove him wrong, with stories such as the one above, the person explained what he meant. When Jesus met this woman, he did not see a prostitute. When Jesus meets any person, he does not see that person identified with sin. When Jesus looked at this woman, he saw a child of God, made in his image, who had been sinned against, and sure, had sinned herself. When Jesus looked at this woman, he did not see "damaged goods." he saw a beautiful child of God, whose beauty had been temporarily marred because of what had been done to her as well as by what she had done.

When Jesus looks at you and me, when he considers the damage that has been done to us, that has twisted us, and influenced our behavior and choices, he does not condemn us. He is familiar – perhaps more than any of us because of his divine perspective and the experience of the cross – with what sin can do to a person. The prophet Isaiah said just that, in a prophecy about Jesus:

> *He was despised and rejected by men, a man of sorrows, and familiar with suffering. Like one from whom men hide their faces he was despised, and we esteemed him not.*
> *(Isaiah 53:3)*

It is often true in life that those who hurt others have often been deeply hurt themselves. Hurt people hurt people. The reality is that Jesus is able to look beyond what has been done to us and see the beauty of what remains, even if it appears ugly to us. Thus, in this story, he broke another social taboo by praising a woman in public, and what's worse (!), he praised her above a man of high social status. In Jesus' evaluation, the broken, repentant former prostitute was worthy of praise, whereas the snooty, self-righteous Pharisee deserved rebuke.

Throughout the gospels, we see those who are broken, those who are wounded, those who are aware of their own failures flocking to Jesus. There is no condemnation in his eyes for those whose hearts are heavy because they have been sinned against, and in turn, have sinned themselves. It is the unbroken, the proud, the self-righteous who are wary and (rightly) afraid to approach him. The broken ones need have no fear.

In the end, we need to understand that Jesus does not see us primarily as victims, or even as perpetrators of evil. With a divine "double vision," he is able to see who we truly are as children of God, though perhaps temporarily marred, and who we can become under his tender care.

Donna's bear

When my sister Donna was young, we used to take walks along the beach in Herne Bay, England. Our house was about 3 minutes from the beach, and it was easy entertainment. One day as we were walking along, Donna ran down to the edge of the water and pulled out a gray, soggy mass from the waves. On closer inspection, we determined that it was once a white teddy bear, but now it was a dirty mess, caked in oil, seaweed and other unsavory elements from the sea. We urged Donna to throw it back in the water, since it was clearly without value and beyond redemption, but she stubbornly refused, insisting that it could be cleaned up and made good again.

Under protest, we took it home, and my mother, being a good sport and indulging Donna's fantasy future for this ruined toy, put it in the washing machine with a good helping of detergent. To our great surprise, after a cycle in the washing machine and a quick bout in the tumble dryer, the teddy bear had amazingly regained all of its former glory. It was white, soft, and definitely worth cuddling.

I learned a lesson from that experience. I had written that teddy bear off. I had thought it was too damaged and too dirty to ever be good again. Donna had something like that divine "double vision." She saw what it was, but she also saw what it could become with some care and cleaning. Despite the abuse it had suffered, it could be redeemed. It could be made beautiful again.

Now we may be tempted to think of ourselves like that bear in its former condition: thrown around through the storms and circumstances of life, abused, dirty, without value and beyond redemption. But in God's hands, with some care and cleaning, we can become beautiful again, and definitely worth cuddling!

But you were washed, you were sanctified, you were justified in the name of the Lord Jesus Christ and by the Spirit of our God. (1 Corinthians 6:11b)

Truth and a Prayer

I am not my past.

I am not what has been done to me.

In God's eyes, I am his child, and I can be beautiful and clean again.

Dear God, my Father in heaven,
Thank you that you see me with a divine double vision, as I am, but also as I can be. Cleanse me from what has been done to me, and what I have done in response. Make me a new creation, beautiful in your eyes. Let your truth about me be the only truth that matters. Help me see myself as you see me.
In Jesus' Name,
Amen.

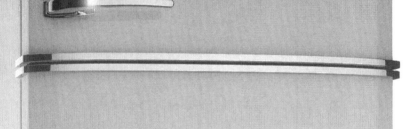

CHAPTER
7

SINNER: WHAT HAVE I DONE (TO MYSELF, TO OTHERS)?

This next story bridges the last chapter to this one, in that it involves a person who is definitely sinned against, but also has made her own poor choices and is reaping the consequences. We find the story in John chapter 8:

8 But Jesus went to the Mount of Olives. 2 At dawn he appeared again in the temple courts, where all the people gathered around him, and he sat down to teach them. 3 The teachers of the law and the Pharisees brought in a woman caught in adultery. They made her stand before the group 4 and said to Jesus, "Teacher, this woman was caught in the act of adultery. 5 In the Law Moses commanded us to stone such women. Now what do you say?" 6 They were using this question as a trap, in order to have a basis for accusing him.

But Jesus bent down and started to write on the ground with his finger. 7 When they kept on questioning him, he straightened up and said to them, "If any one of you is without sin, let him be the first to throw a stone at her." 8 Again he stooped down and wrote on the ground.

9 At this, those who heard began to go away one at a time, the older ones first, until only Jesus was left, with the woman still standing there. 10 Jesus straightened up and asked her, "Woman, where are they? Has no one condemned you?"

11 "No one, sir," she said.

"Then neither do I condemn you," Jesus declared. "Go now and leave your life of sin."

Let's consider first how she is sinned against. For the teachers of the Law and the Pharisees, who bring her before Jesus, she is nothing more than a pawn in their chess game against him. She is an opening gambit, a bargaining counter that they are willing to use to make their point and then discard like a used Kleenex once she has served their purpose. They are uneven in their application of the Law, in that the Law of Moses stated that both the man and the woman should face consequences for their adultery, but somehow, the man seems to have escaped this fate. To them she is a mere object, a tool for their use.

Not so for Jesus. He seems to be caught on the horns of a dilemma. It looks as though he has only two choices: he could uphold the Law of Moses and condone the stoning of the woman, but if he does so, he would lose his reputation for compassion and as a man of the people. He would have the death of this woman on his conscience. He could possibly also incur the wrath of the Romans, since the Jews were forbidden from exercising the death penalty by themselves. On the other hand, if he refuses to condone the stoning of the woman, he risks being seen as opposed to the Law of Moses and being branded a heretic. It looks like an impossible dilemma. Both options get Jesus in trouble.

With characteristic brilliance, Jesus finds a third option. He admits that the woman deserves the penalty but issues a condition that only someone who is without sin can cast the first stone. One by one, they drop their stones, the older ones first, perhaps more conscious of their years of sin and without the arrogance of youth. With his words, Jesus forces them to face their own guilt and class themselves as sinners along with this woman. From first seeing themselves as above and superior to her, Jesus brings them to the uncomfortable realization that they, too, have fallen far short of what God requires of their lives.

The irony here is that there is one there who is without sin and who would be qualified to throw the first stone: Jesus himself - but he is the only one who does not want to. He acts in splendid defense of the woman, and her accusers disperse. The crowd was bursting with self-righteous condemnation, but now, deflated, they slink away. Only Jesus and the woman are left. He has, quite literally, saved her life.

What is interesting here is that he does not avoid the sin issue. Though Jesus is not willing to condemn her, he is also not willing to leave her in her sin. He utters this important phrase: "Go now and leave your life of sin." Within these eight words is a powerful message. Jesus acknowledges that she has sinned, that there is damage she has done to herself, and which is an offense to God. However, with the words, "leave your life of sin," he communicates the liberating message that she is both able and capable of living differently. He communicates his belief in her ability to make better choices, to live a more moral life, and to honor God with her sexuality.

When Jesus looks at us, he sees the reality of our sin, the ways in which we fall short, but he does not condemn. In fact, he cannot condemn those who have placed their trust in him:

> *8 Therefore, there is now no condemnation for those who are in Christ Jesus ... (Romans 8:1a)*

In the verse that follows the best-known verse in the Bible, Jesus says of himself:

17 For God did not send his Son into the world to condemn the world, but to save the world through him. (John 3:17)[1]

In his eyes we do not find condemnation, but belief – belief in his power to transform a life; belief in our ability to cooperate with him in this act of transformation; belief that we can live differently. And that makes a difference. We need not be identified with our failures, our mistakes, our poor choices. Instead, he invites us to move toward a better future. He invites us to a better "us," not through willpower or determination, but through surrender to him.

Hebrews 2 and 4

It is not that Jesus is unaware of our sin. As God in the flesh, he is well aware of the offense that sin is against his holiness; but he does not stand above humanity, in distant condemnation. He stands with us, in the dirt and difficulty of the human condition, and knows what it is like to be human. He understands what it is to struggle with sin. The writer to the Hebrews confirms that when he says:

14 Since the children have flesh and blood, he too shared in their humanity so that by his death he might destroy him who holds the power of death - that is, the devil - 15 and free those who all their lives were held in slavery by their fear of death. 16 For surely it is not angels he helps, but Abraham's descendants. 17 For this reason he had to be made like his brothers in every way, in order that he might

---

[1] Some commentators believe that this sentence is from John, the gospel writer, rather than Jesus himself, but it makes no difference to the point.

become a merciful and faithful high priest in service to God, and that he might make atonement for the sins of the people. 18 Because he himself suffered when he was tempted, he is able to help those who are being tempted.
(Hebrews 2:14-18)

Note the key phrases here: "he shared in their humanity ... made like his brothers in every way ... He himself suffered when he was tempted." This is in stark contrast to how we usually think about Jesus. Although we may count ourselves as theologically orthodox in understanding him to be "fully God and fully man," I think that most of us think he had some sort of inherent advantage against temptation. We imagine that when temptation strolls up to him, he opens his wallet, flashes his "Son of God" card, and temptation retreats, hastily apologizing. What utter nonsense! Apparently, he "suffered" when he was tempted, which to me means that he thought about it. He considered it; he battled against it, and he won the battle, but it was not easy.

The same idea is communicated in Hebrews 4:

14 Therefore, since we have a great high priest who has gone through the heavens, Jesus the Son of God, let us hold firmly to the faith we profess. 15 For we do not have a high priest who is unable to sympathize with our weaknesses, but we have one who has been tempted in every way, just as we are - yet was without sin. 16 Let us then approach the throne of grace with confidence, so that we may receive mercy and find grace to help us in our time of need.

There it is again: "not ... unable to sympathize with our weaknesses ... tempted in every way, just as we are ...," and the exhortation of the writer is entirely consistent with that understanding. We can approach the throne of grace with confidence. We do not need to approach God like cowering dogs afraid of another beating. We can talk confidently to God, knowing that we will find mercy and grace in abundance.

Zacchaeus

Let's move on to another notorious sinner in the New Testament: Zacchaeus. Some background historical knowledge is necessary in order for us to understand exactly why he was so despised. After a period of self-rule during the time of the Maccabees, the Jewish nation had become subjugated to the occupying power of Rome. The Romans were the hated occupiers, and their practice was to conquer, occupy the country and then tax the population.

Then, as now, taxes were not popular – but it gets worse. Rather than collect the taxes themselves, and face verbal and worse abuse from the Jewish population, they enlisted representatives from the Jewish nation themselves to become their tax collectors. They were given a quota of taxes to collect, and anything additional they managed to squeeze from the population was theirs to keep. As you can imagine, that was not a popular occupation, but for those who were prepared to face the ire and disgust of their fellow countrymen, it could be a lucrative endeavor.

To give a more modern interpretation of the response such a tax collector would receive, imagine a French national, living in Paris in 1941. The Germans invaded the country in June of the previous year. Instead of remaining neutral, or joining the French resistance, he chooses to work for the Nazis and raise money for their cause, and a little extra for himself. Can you imagine how he would be viewed by his fellow countrymen? As a traitor, and even worse, someone who is profiting from their misfortune and collaborating with the hated occupying power. Such is the reputation of Zacchaeus, who is not only a tax collector, but a *chief* tax collector, who has others working for him in this despicable trade. This is how Luke tells of his encounter with Jesus:

> *19 Jesus entered Jericho and was passing through. 2 A man was there by the name of Zacchaeus; he was a chief tax collector and was wealthy. 3 he wanted to see who Jesus was, but being a short man he could not, because of the crowd. 4 So he ran ahead and climbed a sycamore-fig tree to see him, since Jesus was coming that way.*

> *5 When Jesus reached the spot, he looked up and said to him, "Zacchaeus, come down immediately. I must stay at your house today." 6 So he came down at once and welcomed him gladly.*

> *7 All the people saw this and began to mutter, "He has gone to be the guest of a 'sinner.'"*

> *8 But Zacchaeus stood up and said to the Lord, "Look, Lord! here and now I give half of my possessions to the poor, and if I have cheated anybody out of anything, I will pay back four times the amount."*

> *9 Jesus said to him, "Today salvation has come to this house, because this man, too, is a son of Abraham. 10 For the Son of Man came to seek and to save what was lost." (Luke 19:1-10)*

Excuse me? What is going on here? At the very least you might expect Jesus to do the decent thing and shun Zacchaeus, ignore him, walk on by. After all, Jesus is starting to look very much like the Messiah, and a common expectation of the Messiah was that he would oust the Romans from their land. The Jews following him would certainly expect a reaction to Zacchaeus in keeping with that expectation. But this? Jesus invites himself to dinner?

In that culture, the symbolism of hospitality was enormous. By inviting himself to dinner with Zacchaeus, Jesus is saying much more than just that he is hungry and Zacchaeus will be able to provide him a meal. To share a meal with someone in that culture implies intimacy, friendship, relationship. The common phrase for disreputable people at that time was "sinners and tax collectors," and here Jesus is, planning to sit down for a nice meal with a traitorous collaborator, an evil tool of the occupying Roman Empire. It is astonishing and completely unexpected - not least by Zacchaeus, who is so surprised and overwhelmed by this implied offer of relationship that he bursts into a speech of repentance and planned restitution.

I think it's important to note the sequence here. It is not that Jesus had dinner with Zacchaeus, confronted him with his sin, explained the path of salvation, and as a response Zacchaeus repents. No. The offer of relationship comes first. Jesus' unconditional acceptance of this man, who even by his own standards was a scoundrel, is completely overwhelming and elicits this amazing response.

So how does this relate to us? We may think of ourselves as traitors to the cause. There may have been a time when we aligned ourselves wholeheartedly with the people of God and the cause of Christ, but then we turned away, and perhaps even despised the things for which we were formerly so enthusiastic. We may have mocked Christians. We may have mocked Christ, if not with words, then with a life lived so contrary to what we know he wanted for us.

Even traitors have a chance of return, though. Even Peter, who denied Christ three times, was given the offer of restoration to relationship, and he grasped it eagerly. What about you? Will you return to the One who offers relationship to you, who is willing to embrace a traitor, willing to accept back someone who has denied him? his arms are open. He does not condemn or accuse. He invites.

The Prodigal Son

Perhaps the best-known story of a sinner who is welcomed back is the story of the Prodigal Son. This story contains so much truth that represents the whole gospel that it is known as "the gospel within the gospel." Though you may be familiar with it, bear with me, and read it through one more time ...

11 Jesus continued: "There was a man who had two sons. 12 The younger one said to his father, 'Father, give me my share of the estate.' So he divided his property between them.

13 "Not long after that, the younger son got together all he had, set off for a distant country and there squandered his wealth in wild living. 14 After he had spent everything, there was a severe famine in that whole country, and he began to be in need. 15 So he went and hired himself out to a citizen of that country, who sent him to his fields to feed pigs. 16 he longed to fill his stomach with the pods that the pigs were eating, but no one gave him anything.

17 "When he came to his senses, he said, 'How many of my father's hired men have food to spare, and here I am starving to death! 18 I will set out and go back to my father and say to him: Father, I have sinned against heaven and against you. 19 I am no longer worthy to be called your son; make me like one of your hired men.' 20 So he got up and went to his father.

"But while he was still a long way off, his father saw him and was filled with compassion for him; he ran to his son, threw his arms around him and kissed him.

21 "The son said to him, 'Father, I have sinned against heaven and against you. I am no longer worthy to be called your son.'

22 "But the father said to his servants, 'Quick! Bring the best robe and put it on him. Put a ring on his finger and sandals on his feet. 23 Bring the fattened calf and kill it. Let's have a feast and celebrate. 24 For this son of mine was dead and is alive again; he was lost and is found.' So they began to celebrate. (Luke 15:11-24)

In this story, the father is somewhat representative of the heavenly Father, God himself, and the prodigal, or wasteful, son represents any of us who have turned away from God and gone our own way. The representation is not exact, however, and the differences are important, as we will see shortly.

The son is not satisfied with his existence, despite being in close relationship with his father. He is searching for something more ("the grass is greener" syndrome?) and requests his inheritance early. As Kenneth Bailey points out in his excellent book, *Poet & Peasant and Through Peasant Eyes*, the first listeners to this story would have expected the father to beat the son for his audacity in requesting his inheritance. It implies that he is more interested in getting the money than in his father continuing to live a long and healthy life. A surprise element is that the father accedes to his request and lets him go. It does not take long for the son to reach rock bottom, eking out a meager existence feeding pigs for a Gentile farmer. For a Jewish boy, you can't go much lower than that.

In his distress, he finally comes to his senses and realizes that he would be much better off at home – but can he return home? Would he be accepted back, or has he burned that bridge forever? With desperate hope, he prepares a speech with three components:

a) an acknowledgment of his wrongdoing: "Father, I have sinned against heaven (God) and against you";

b) an acknowledgment of what he deserves: "I am no longer worthy to be called your son," and

c) an offer to pay back what he has wasted, through being hired by his father (the presumption is that his wages would go toward repayment).

I can imagine the long walk home, with the son rehearsing the speech to make sure he got it exactly right, attempting to secure his chances of being accepted back, albeit at a much lower social status than as a son and heir of the father. As he approaches the village, his father, who has been looking for him, sees him, is filled with compassion and runs to him.

In seminary, I remember my principal, Peter Cotterell, speaking on this passage and saying, "I'm glad my heavenly Father did a lot better than that!" In contrast to the father in this story, who is somewhat passive, confining himself to looking longingly out of the window and hoping for his son to return, our heavenly Father sent his own Son on a rescue mission to bring us back. It was a mission that involved a movement from heaven to earth in the form of the Incarnation (a downgrade, if ever there was one!) and that would take his Son to an agonizing death on a cross. That's how far the heavenly Father will go to ensure our safe return and guarantee our welcome home.

There is another surprise in the story, which many Western readers might miss. The father *runs* to the son. So what? There are a couple of things to understand here. A Middle-Eastern father would not run. He would walk slowly in a dignified manner. Children run. A respected patriarch of the family and pillar of the village would not run. To run would be completely undignified and humiliating. Yet he runs. Why?

We could put it down to simple enthusiasm, but there is almost certainly a deeper reason. This culture is very much a "shame culture" compared to most Western cultures, which are "guilt cultures." What this means is that social behavior is primarily governed not by individual conscience but by how one's actions will be perceived by others. In the interconnected society of the New Testament, when the son left the village, he did not just go on his own account. He went as a representative of the village, and his disgraceful actions have brought shame upon them all.

To give a modern example, imagine a boy living in a small West Virginia town where traditionally all of the men have worked in the coal mines. Through diligence and hard work, the boy gets the opportunity to go to college, and if he does so, he would be the first one from that small town. The problem is that his family cannot afford the cost of his housing and tuition. However, the townspeople rally around and scrape together enough money, though it is a great sacrifice, to support him for his first year, and off he goes.

Soon though, reports come back to the town that all has not gone well. The boy has dropped out of college, lost the one scholarship he had, and spends most of his days smoking pot and his nights getting drunk at parties. The money that the townspeople gave him is gone, wasted on drugs and alcohol. Now he is on his way home, and they are waiting for him at the Greyhound bus stop. Can you imagine the reception he would receive? Now you get the picture.

Back to the first century ...

It is highly likely that without the father's swift intervention, the son would have had to "run the gauntlet" of village men, outraged at him and willing to deal him a few violent blows as a physical reprimand for his actions. Seen in that light, the father's swift move to him can be seen as a protective act rather than simply enthusiasm for the returning boy.

Let's consider the speech that the boy prepared. If you remember, it was supposed to contain admission of wrongdoing, acknowledgment of what he deserves and his plan for repayment of the debt. As it happens, the son can only get out the first two sentences before he is engulfed in his father's embrace and gets a mouthful of robe!

In Jesus' telling of the story, the son never manages to present his plan for repayment, and I think that is very deliberate. Although the father allows the son's acknowledgment of his sin, he contradicts the son's assessment of what he deserves. The son claims that he is no longer worthy to be called a son, yet the father immediately restores his status by calling for a robe to be put on him, and sandals on his feet. Bare feet belonged to slaves and hired workers, and the presence of the robe and footwear would indicate to the whole village that the son was to be restored to his former status, rather than be demoted to slave or hired worker. In fact, the son doesn't even get so far as to present that plan to his father. It becomes totally unnecessary, because the father's lavish display of grace and forgiveness says all that needs to be said.

In the end, the son's situation is ours. We are unable to repay our debt to God, to put right our rebellion, to pay the cost of our sin. It is beyond us. Out of pride, we might wish to believe that we could make some adequate recompense, but we cannot. Ultimately, we are utterly dependent on the grace and mercy of our heavenly Father and the forgiveness won for us by his Son Jesus on the cross. Only the cross can deal with our guilt and shame. Only that sacrifice can return us to right relationship with the Father.

The parallels are clear: We do not have a father who lets us go and then forgets about us. We have one who longs for our return and will even go so far as to send his dearly loved Son to rescue us, even though it will cost that Son his life. When we return, conscious of our failure and with our heads hung low with shame, it is not a beating that we receive but an unexpected and delightful hug. We are not grudgingly accepted back as slaves or servants, but restored as a sons or daughters to the Father. Rather than our return being a huge embarrassment, it is the cause of great celebration. We were lost, but now are found, and we can hold our tear-stained heads high as we walk the street in the close embrace of the Father.

Revelation 12: The Accuser

It would be wonderful if the story ended there. It would, except for the inconvenient fact that we have an enemy, namely Satan, who detests anyone feeling like a loved, forgiven, beautiful, accepted child of God. Rather than let us live in the light of our forgiveness, he will do his best to remind us of our failures, with the goal of so diminishing our self-esteem that we believe we can never be useful to God, or that perhaps we don't even belong in this redeemed family. The very word "Satan" means "accuser," and that is his specialty. We read about his evil scheme in Revelation 12:

10 Then I heard a loud voice in heaven say:

"Now have come the salvation and the power and the kingdom of our God,
*   and the authority of his Christ.*
For the accuser of our brothers,
*   who accuses them before our God day and night,*
*   has been hurled down.*
11 They overcame him
*   by the blood of the Lamb*
*   and by the word of their testimony;*
They did not love their lives so much
*   as to shrink from death. (Revelation 12:10-11)*

The accuser of our brothers (and sisters, though the Bible, written in a patriarchal context, will default to the masculine) accuses them before God day and night. Satan, the accuser, attempts to persuade God that we are unworthy, that he does not want us, that he would be better without us - but he does not succeed. Though his recounting of our sins may be accurate, they have been dealt with by "the blood of the Lamb," i.e., the sacrifice of Christ on the cross. That, combined with "the word of their testimony," i.e., our statement of our allegiance to Christ and his power in our lives, and our willingness to "not love [our] lives" but abandon them to his cause, is sufficient to hurl down the accuser and overcome him.

Even the foreshadowing of the cross in the Old Testament declares the efficacy of a blood sacrifice to deal with sin:

> ... *as far as the east is from the west,*
>   *so far has he removed our transgressions from us.*
> *13 As a father has compassion on his children,*
>   *so the Lord has compassion on those who fear him;*
> *(Psalm 103:12-13)*

And this:

> *"Come now, let us reason together," says the LORD.*
> *"Though your sins are like scarlet, they shall be as white as*
> *snow; though they are red as crimson, they shall be like*
> *wool." (Isaiah 1:18)*

And this:

> *"No longer will a man teach his neighbor, or a man his brother, saying, 'Know the LORD,' because they will all know me, from the least of them to the greatest," declares the LORD. "For I will forgive their wickedness and will remember their sins no more." (Jeremiah 31:34)*

Our transgressions are removed as far as the East is from the West. Our sins, once scarlet, are now covered, and white as snow. Our wickedness is remembered no more.

What that means is that God has decided to forget our sin, not because he suffers from poor memory, but because he has "divine amnesia," a chosen ability to cast our sin from his mind, and be unable to recall it. The staggering implication of that is that if I genuinely repent of my sin, if I am truly sorry and say so to God, then it is forgiven and forgotten. If I made such a genuine confession and repentance, and then 30 minutes later came back to God to repent of the same thing, he would effectively say, "I don't know what you are talking about. I have no record of that."

In 1 John, the apostle provides us with both a reality check and a wonderful promise:

> *8 If we claim to be without sin, we deceive ourselves and the truth is not in us. 9 If we confess our sins, he is faithful and just and will forgive us our sins and purify us from all unrighteousness. (1 John 1:8-9)*

Notice here that he is very clear that we cannot be in denial about our sin. Our first step in dealing with sin is admission of it. When we do admit it, though, and when we do confess it, the promise is clear: he will forgive us, and will purify us, from *all* unrighteousness. Not some. All. When Jesus cleanses us, he does it perfectly. We are fully cleaned up, fully forgiven, fully acceptable to the father.

For some of us, our sin, and perhaps the sin committed against us, has left us feeling dirty. There's a sense of shame, some deserved and some perhaps not. In either case, in bringing it to Jesus, we can be purified. We can be made clean, fresh and new. The apostle Paul, writing to the Corinthian church said:

> *Therefore, if anyone is in Christ, he is a new creation; the old has gone, the new has come! (2 Corinthians 5:17)*

Now that is good news. Perhaps for us, this being "born again" brings with it a return to innocence, like that of a baby. We can have a soul that is renewed, and although some of those soul scars might never fully disappear, to God, we appear perfect.

Tetelestai

That brings me to my favorite word in the Bible. It's a Greek word, and it's found in the Gospel of John. Jesus is on the cross, near the point of death. He says that he is thirsty, and someone gives him a drink …

> *30 When he had received the drink, Jesus said, "It is finished." With that, he bowed his head and gave up his spirit. (John 19:30)*

The English words "It is finished," in Greek, are a single word: *tetelestai*.

To fully understand the depths of the theological

significance of this phrase, we need to know something about the culture and what the hearers would have understood by it. It was not simply that the ordeal was over, that the hours of torturous endurance on the cross were over. The word *tetelestai* was a word used in accounting and on receipts. It was written on a bill or a business document to indicate something that was "Paid in Full."

When Jesus uttered these words on the cross, what he meant would have been clear to those standing around. He meant that whatever debt we had accrued to God because of our sin, whatever price was required to put things right, it was now Paid in Full.

Think about that. In FULL. Not a partial payment with something required from me to make up the balance. Not dependent on something else from me.

Simply... paid ... in ... full

Peter Maiden of Operation Mobilization once said, "When I look at the cross, I relax. Because I know that God is no longer angry at me." What a beautiful truth. God has nothing against us any more. His fully justified, fully understandable anger at sin, because of his holy nature that cannot abide it, is dealt with, appeased and satisfied by his Son, who took the punishment in our place.

Though we may sometimes *feel* guilty, *feel* unworthy, *feel* that God may hold something against us, the fact is that he does not. It really is finished. And it is in the fact of that completed work that we must place our trust.

I sometimes counsel people who fear that some horrendous sin they have committed is not forgiven. After offering appropriate pastoral consolation and understanding, I challenge them with the import of what they are saying, and if I'm feeling bold, will often ask:

"So, do you really think this sin, your one particular sin, is so special, so unique, so particularly horrendous, that it is bigger than the cross? Do you really think that Jesus could take care of the sins of the whole world throughout all of history, past, present and future, but get stuck on yours? Do you think your sin is that special and unique? Doesn't that seem a bit arrogant?"

Then they may feel a little guilty about the sin of arrogance, but if that's what it takes to cure bad theology, I'm prepared to risk it!

Developing the accounting metaphor a little further, we come to a delightful theological concept called "imputation." For this word, though, we're going to need the King James translation:

11 And he received the sign of circumcision, a seal of the righteousness of the faith which he had yet being uncircumcised: that he might be the father of all them that believe, though they be not circumcised; that righteousness might be imputed unto them also (Romans 4:11)

This verse refers to Abraham as the father of all who believe, but by virtue of his faith rather than by any action on his part. As a result of his faith, righteousness is "imputed" to him and to us also, as those who, in the same vein as Abraham's faith in God, believe by faith in Jesus and what he achieved for us on the cross. What that means in accounting terms is that all the goodness and righteousness of Jesus are imputed, or credited, to us, and all the sin and wickedness that we have ever done or thought are credited to him. What a transaction! I call it The Great Exchange. All of my "badness" is put in his column, and all of his "goodness" is placed in mine. Now, to the Father, I look as good as his own Son, clothed in his righteousness.

In his famous hymn, "And Can It Be," hymn writer Charles Wesley put it this way:

> *No condemnation now I dread;*
> *Jesus, and all in him, is mine;*
> *Alive in him, my living head,*
> *And clothed in righteousness divine,*
> *Bold I approach the eternal throne,*
> *And claim the crown, through Christ my own.*
> *Bold I approach the eternal throne,*
> *And claim the crown, through Christ my own.*

Tetelestai. It is finished!

Truth and a Prayer:

It is forgiven.
It is forgotten.
It is finished.

Lord Jesus,
Thank you that through your sacrifice, my sins are dealt with, forgiven and forgotten. Though the enemy may accuse me, though my conscience may trouble me, let me rest in the knowledge that God is not angry with me. You love me, and I welcome your peace into my soul.
In Jesus' Name,
Amen.

A Different Prayer

In a general sense we are all God's children. He is the Creator, and we are the created, but he wants us to know him in a deeper sense. He wants us to be in relationship with him, knowing him as Father, as Lord and Savior, and as Spirit. Having read this chapter, you may have discovered within yourself a desire to experience this forgiveness, this sense of "it is finished" for yourself. For centuries, people have called out to God, acknowledging their need of him, acknowledging the sacrifice Jesus made on the cross for their sins. God offers us this gift of acceptance and salvation. All we need do is open our hands to receive this gift. If you have never done that and wish to do so, you can use the following as a prayer, or as the basis for your own words to God:

God, I acknowledge that you made me and you love me. By my sin I have separated myself from you, but I don't want to continue like that. I understand that on the cross Jesus paid the price for my sin and that he extends an offer of relationship to me. I accept him now as my Savior and ask you, God, to come into my heart, to make me your child. Lead me by your Spirit. Help me live a life pleasing to you. Help me live in the light of your incredible love for me.
In Jesus' Name,
Amen.

If you just prayed that prayer for the first time, then the Bible says that angels are rejoicing in heaven! You have been the cause of a party! In Bible words, you have been transferred from the kingdom of darkness into the kingdom of light. Your next step, if you are not already part of a church, is to seek a group of believers with whom you can grow as a young Christian. Search for a church and/or small group, meet some people, tell them that you prayed to receive Christ, and ask them what you should do next. If they don't have any good answers, move on to a group that does!

You'll find that Christianity, which in its essence means living like Jesus, was never designed to be a solitary pursuit, but that God desires us to be in a family of faith, where we can be encouraged, and picked up when we fall. Search hard for such a place, and when you find it, commit yourself to it.

Also, a personal request: If you did pray that prayer, would you shoot me an e-mail and let me know. It would be a tremendous personal encouragement to me. Here's my e-mail address:

glynnorman@gmail.com

Thank you – and welcome to the most exciting journey of your life, both in this life and the eternal life that Jesus promised.

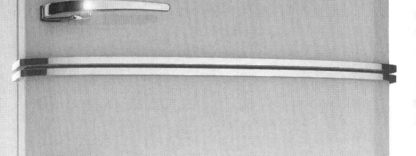

CHAPTER

8

WHAT AM I REALLY WORTH?

I think I was about 8 years old, at least old enough to walk to school with a group of friends rather than be escorted by my mum. One day as we were walking, a friend of mine saw some rocks lying by the side of the path. With enthusiasm, he suggested that we throw them as high as we could against the tall wall that ran alongside the path. The wall was probably 10 or 12 feet tall, and my guess was that I would be able to get it near the top. As it turned out, I had underestimated my own strength, and the rock went sailing over the wall. All we heard was a dull thud as it landed, and then a shout. We turned and ran, but not quickly enough.

A college student came through a gate and quickly caught up with us, wanting to know who had thrown the rock that had hit his car. My friends quickly gave me up as the culprit, and the interrogation ensued. Apparently, the rock had left a significant dent in the student's car. I had no money to pay for the repair, so the best I could do was give him my address. I went home that afternoon and told my parents what had happened. That night he turned up at our house, and after a brief discussion with my father, left with payment for the repair in his pocket.

It was embarrassing. I was guilty. I had no excuse. I had no means to put right the damage I had caused. I was utterly dependent on my father to remedy the situation. The more astute readers will already recognize this story as a setup, in that it neatly expresses some of the core truths about our relationship with God. The rocks we have thrown, the Bible calls "sin," and many times, it is not accidental. We created a situation we could not remedy. We could not fix what we had broken. Only

God could put it right, and at great personal cost to himself, he did so.

Worth dying for

This is the bottom line: what are you worth? How does God see you? In the end, those are the most important questions we have encountered in this book. Although other sources have spoken into our self-image (family, society, our own view of ourselves), it is God's voice that we must allow to prevail. It is his estimation of us that we must accept as valid, above all other opinions.

The amazing fact is that God considers each of us worth dying for – not out of any inherent merit that we bring to the equation, but simply because he loves us as his children. This is what the Bible says about it:

> *6 You see, at just the right time, when we were still powerless, Christ died for the ungodly. 7 Very rarely will anyone die for a righteous man, though for a good man someone might possibly dare to die. 8 But God demonstrates his own love for us in this: While we were still sinners, Christ died for us. (Romans 5:6-8)*

Think about this: In those two verses we are called both "ungodly" and "sinners." In our very nature, we are opposed to God. In our thoughts and our actions we rebel against him. Earlier in the Book of Romans, Paul describes us as "God-haters" … and yet. And yet, even in the middle of our rebellion, our abuse, our turning our backs on him, God's love for us burns so strongly that he will not leave us in that sorry state. He will do whatever it takes to restore us to relationship to him. Whatever it takes.

Before I became a father, I understood the concept of God giving his Son in a mostly theoretical way. I understood it somewhat, and was thankful for it, but then becoming a father to a baby boy changed that perspective. Suddenly I understood that what God was allowing to die in my place was his Baby Boy. I understood that his fatherly affection for his Son was certainly no less than my affection for my son, and presumably much more, since it is not tarnished by the limitations of sin or humanity. How deep is his love for us! As Stuart Townend's song says:

How deep the Father's love for us,
How vast beyond all measure,
That he should give his only Son
To make a wretch his treasure.

How great the pain of searing loss,
The Father turns his face away,
As wounds which mar the chosen One
Bring many sons to glory.

When I consider how much I would need to love someone to let my own son die in order to restore my relationship with that person, I cannot imagine it. The fiercest and strongest love I feel for my son may be only a microcosm of the love relationship the Father has with his Son, the One who has been with him forever in the closest, most intimate Father-Son relationship possible.

However, because he loves me, God was willing to let his own Son die – that he might take the punishment that I deserved – and thus make it possible for me to be restored to relationship with him.

If I had to complete such a transaction, I doubt I could do it. I cannot imagine loving another person so much that I would give up my son. If I did do it, I think I would always resent the person who made such a transaction necessary. Because of what that individual did, my father's heart would be broken. Could I ever forgive the person for that?

The comparison is not perfect, since the skeptical side of me is forced to consider the fact that God knew that he would get his Son back, that he would return to life in three days. So, although he was submitting himself to short-term loss and pain, he was assured of a happy ending. However, I think that analysis fails to appreciate the depths of the disconnect that the Father and Son experienced during that time.

They had been in the closest of all intimate relationships, for all time. They had experienced an unbroken unity and togetherness from all eternity. Yet now, through the Crucifixion, two horrific emotional and spiritual consequences occur. Their deep soul intimacy is shattered, as he who knew no sin becomes sin for us – and in that moment, becomes separated from God the Father, feeling, for the first time ever, utterly alone and abandoned. In that moment of soul crushing despair, he cries out in the words of Psalm 22:1: "My God, My God, why have you forsaken me?"

From the Father's perspective, to have to turn your back on his own son at the son's most desperate time must have been heartbreaking. In addition to that, he endures hours of watching his precious boy being scourged with whips, beaten and impaled on a cross, where he struggles to catch his breath as life ebbs from him. Six hours he was on that cross, six hours when everything in the Father's heart must have longed to intervene, to put an end to the torture and suffering. Yet he allowed it, because of his love for me - and because of his love for you.

I remember one time when I was "forced" to endure the suffering of one of my children. When my daughter Cicely was 3 years old, she was knocked over by a goat in a petting zoo, and as she fell, she gashed her head on a log and split the skin open. We rushed her to a pediatric urgent care facility, and they did their best to numb the area around the wound prior to stitching it. My wife was in the room with her, as my son and I waited outside. Despite their best attempts at numbing, my daughter could still feel the stitches being put in, and screamed at the top of her lungs at the pain. I felt utterly helpless and frustrated that I could (or rather, should) do nothing about it, because the end result would be worth what she was enduring. However, those 10 minutes of hearing my little girl scream were emotionally agonizing for me.

Yes, the Father would eventually get his Son back, but he would watch him in pain for six long hours, and for the plan to work, not be able to do anything about it. Yes, he would get him back, but before then there would be an accusation of abandonment and a spiritual gulf between them that is hard to imagine in contrast with the closeness of their former connection.

So great is the Father's love for us that he would endure this, that we might be restored in relationship to him.

God rejoices over you with singing

There is a saying that to err is human and to forgive is divine – and that is the astonishing truth. Even though we made necessary the death of his Son, God does not resent us. He does not despise us or look upon us with anger. Zephaniah the prophet records words to the nation Israel, which we can easily appropriate for ourselves. They were a nation grown distant from God. We are individuals, but his sentiment toward us remains the same:

> *The Lord your God is with you,*
> *he is mighty to save.*
> *He will take great delight in you,*
> *he will quiet you with his love,*
> *he will rejoice over you with singing. (Zephaniah 3:17)*

What beautiful words! God is mighty. He is able to save us from ourselves, even our poor, distorted, hall-of-mirrors view of ourselves. He not only accepts us, he takes great delight in us. Delight is what I imagine children experiencing when they open long-hoped-for presents on Christmas morning. Their face lights up. They are filled with joy. That is exactly what they wanted! It may be hard for you to believe, but you are exactly what God wanted. Not someone else. Not a different, better version of you. Just. You.

I love the phrase, "He will quiet you with his love." The scene I imagine is a distressed child, weeping and anxious. As the father gathers her to his chest, her sobs slowly subside, and she relaxes into his arms, feeling safe and secure, free from harm, the pain diminishing in his embrace.

What do we make of "he will rejoice over you with

singing"? To me that sounds as though there is so much joyous emotion built up inside God that he cannot help himself – he must burst into song and announce with music the return of the lost child.

Delight. Love. Rejoicing. Those are not words of resentment. They are words of a father, ecstatic at the homecoming of the wanderer.

Let's look at one more verse, possibly my favorite in the whole Bible:

> *24 To him who is able to keep you from falling and to present you before his glorious presence without fault and with great joy- 25 to the only God our Savior be glory, majesty, power and authority, through Jesus Christ our Lord, before all ages, now and forevermore! Amen. (Jude 24-25)*

Jesus is able to keep us from falling. He will not drop us or abandon us. He offers us strength to resist temptation. So far, so good, but it gets better. We will be presented before God's glorious presence – here it comes – "without fault and with great joy!" We will stand before God, beautiful in our perfection, and Jesus, as he ushers us forward, will present us "with great joy." We are his prize; we are his jewel; we are his beautiful one, and he is proud to present us to his heavenly Father. There is no shame of association, only pride and ownership. We are his, and he is ours.

The only truly reliable source for our self-image is what God thinks of us

In the end, what God thinks about us, the way God sees us, is the most true thing about us that there is. God is the arbiter of all truth, and if he says we are clean, if he says we are perfect, if he says we are forgiven, and precious and beautiful, and worth singing about – what does it matter what anyone else says or thinks?

My lifelong journey, and one I invite you to, is to more fully grasp and base my self-image on what God thinks about me, and not what anybody else thinks. It does not matter who my family, or society, the accuser, or even my own conscience says I am.

What matters is what God says.

CONCLUSION

I was 25 years old and a student at seminary. In the summers, to earn some extra money, I worked at a residential children's home. The home was occupied by children from 11-17 years old, most of whom had been removed from toxic and extremely unhealthy environments. Many of them had been in trouble with the law. Some were violent, some more quietly hostile; few were trusting or happy. They were indeed "the sinned against."

One day a former resident of the children's home came back to visit. Her name was Nicole, and she was an attractive-looking 15-year-old girl who still had friends in the residential home. As I was there supervising, I overheard her conversation with the other kids. She was telling them that she was having awful trouble sleeping at night, and terrible nightmares.

I asked her if that had started recently, and if anything had changed in her life over the previous few months. She told me that her nightmares had started when she began using a set of Tarot cards that a friend had given her. Knowing that Tarot cards are a gateway to occult involvement, I warned her that she was messing with things that should be left alone, and in a moment of rare boldness, in front of the other children, I offered to pray for her, that the nightmares would stop and that she would be able to sleep well again. The other children looked stunned (this was not a Christian residential home, and I'm betting most of them had never prayed before), but I invited everyone to bow their heads, and I prayed a mighty prayer of spiritual battle for Nicole.

She came back the next morning glowing, and

reported excitedly to the other children and me that, for the first time in months, she had slept through the night. I breathed a quiet sigh of relief that God had answered my prayer (forgive my doubt, Lord!), only to then hear her say that she had gotten rid of the Tarot cards. I told her that was great, and she said that she had given them to a friend. Er... friends don't give friends Tarot cards, but I left that lesson for another time.

We chatted some more later as I walked her out of the building. It was then that she opened up to me and told me that she was HIV+, was suffering from AIDS, and that she had contracted it from a former boyfriend, who knew he was infected but didn't tell her. She told me she realized she would probably die in the not-too-distant future, and asked me if I believed in heaven. That led to a wonderful conversation in which where I was able to talk to her about the reality of heaven and the fact that she was precious in God's sight, even though she had AIDS, even though she had under-age sex, even though she didn't think she was a good person. She seemed to take it all in, and even get excited about the prospect of heaven, where there would be no more pain or suffering.

This is the book I wish I could have given Nicole, to let her see that despite what had been done to her, despite what she had done, she was precious to God, and beautiful in his sight; that she could be washed clean with his forgiveness, and find healing and restoration in a relationship with him. I don't know how the story with Nicole ended. I know that I prayed for her, and I hope one day she will walk up to me on a street in heaven, and say, "Do you remember when we talked about this?"

My hope and my prayer are that as you read this book, you began to see yourself as God sees you. You began to understand how beautiful and precious you are to God. You started to see that you are someone worth singing about, and that God rejoices over you. You understood that if God had a fridge, your picture would be on it!

BOOKS AND BEARS

I had certain people in mind as I wrote this book. They represent anyone who has ever had their self-image wounded, their view of themselves damaged by what life has done to them. I realized that for certain groups of people, this book would be medicine for the soul. As I discussed this with my wife, we talked about teenage children in children's homes, women in battered women's shelters, the homeless ...

For people in these situations and others like them, this book could be a gift that would radically change how they see themselves. It could transform their understanding of their value that has been put into question by what they have experienced.

So, here is my suggestion. Think and pray about who you know who might benefit from this book and buy them a copy (or lend them yours). To truly bring home the impact of Donna's story of the white teddy bear in Chapter 6, you could even give a book and a white teddy bear, and so give them a physical reminder of the fact that in God's eyes they can be beautiful, clean and worth hugging.

I've explored Amazon looking for white bears that remind me of that one, and you can find the best candidates on my "God's fridge" blog post here:

http://godsfridge.wordpress.com/2012/12/14/white-bears

I imagine someone turning up at a children's home or women's shelter with books and bears, and that visit having eternal consequences. Please consider that. This is the message I wanted to share with the world. Please help me share it widely. Thank you.

ALSO BY GLYN NORMAN

Your First Year in Ministry: What They Didn't Teach you in Seminary (2012)

Kindle eBook: http://www.amazon.com/Your-First-Year-Ministry-ebook/dp/B009H9415A

Paperback: https://www.createspace.com/3925312

AMAZON REVIEWS:

Dear Reader,

If you found this book helpful, would you please do me a huge favor and write a brief review on Amazon.com. One or two sentences would be fine. Here's the link to the page:

http://www.amazon.com/Fridge-Your-Picture-Would-ebook/dp/B00BDRMEE4/

My hope is for the message of this book to be shared as widely as possible, and your review will help.

Thank you.

FORTHCOMING BOOKS:

If you wish to be added to the mailing list to be advised of forthcoming books, please email me at glynnorman@gmail.com